Resilient Living

with Dr. Sood

resilientliving.net

Building Resilience for the Difficult Days

A Resilience-Based Stress Reduction (RBSR)
Solution for People with Chronic Health
Conditions and Other Life Challenges, and Caregivers

Amit Sood, MD MSc FACP

Happier Stronger Kinder

ISBN 13: 978-0-9995525-8-2
Imprint Name: Global Center for Resiliency and Wellbeing,
Rochester, MN

Disclaimer

The information in this book is not intended to substitute a health care provider's advice or medical care. Please consult your physician or other health care provider if you are experiencing any symptoms or have questions pertaining to the information contained in this book.

Pure

Remove the dirt
from a lump of mud,
all you are left with is
pure water.

No diagnosis, no adversity,
no blame, no life situation,
can stain or spoil,
your true essence.

Anchor your identity
in the faultless you,
to welcome
hope and healing
as they decorate your path,
to your true state—
Pure.

- Amit Sood, MD November 2019

The Tree Sages

Cut a branch, and they grow another one. Block the light from one side, and they bend the other way. Hurl a stone, and they send you a fruit. Burrow a hole in their bosom, and they help build a nest. Trees teach us a lot about humility, kindness, and resilience.

My mind, however, is a work in progress. I notice the weeds more often than I see the tulips. I spend more time running away from my fears than chasing meaning. My retribution instinct is stronger than my forgiveness commitment.

Presently, my instincts rule my narrative. I want to choose differently. I want to take back control of my story.

I want the meaning that drives my moments to be stronger than the fears that hold my spirit. I wish my eyes keep looking at the light, even on a starless night...particularly on a starless night.

I want my senses to be fully awake—so I can touch, taste, smell, hear, and see, more than I ever have.

I long to feel calm and grateful, to be kind and forgiving to others and self, and to those who have annoyed me. I am hungry for inspiration, hope, and courage. I yearn to rise, not despite, but because of my disruption.

I have no doubt my efforts will heal my wounds, physical and emotional. I trust, the more life I add to my moments, the more moments I will add to my life.

Contents

Hello!

Dear friend,

I am grateful to you for traveling with me for a small part of your life's journey. I cannot even begin to imagine the struggles you or your loved one may have faced or might be facing. As a physician and fellow human, I have cried and laughed with thousands of brave souls as we held hands together through their painful as well as hopeful moments.

In addition to developing a deep respect for their courage, I have come to value the importance of personal resilience—to better cope with an illness, thrive, and even transform because of adversity.

Adversities and illnesses are the times when we lose our sense of control and struggle the most with experiencing positive emotions. But these are also the times when our body and mind are the hungriest for uplifting moments and the gift of predictability.

Three reasons I care so much about building personal resilience amidst ongoing health problems and life's other adversities are:

1. Excessive stress is common among people struggling with chronic health conditions and other life challenges.

2. **Higher resilience correlates with decreased risk of disease progression and recurrence, better physical and emotional health and quality of life, lower risk of hospitalization, and higher overall survival.**

3. Research by my team and others shows that **with just a little effort, you can achieve remarkable growth in resilience.**

Pick any medical challenge or life adversity, resilience will come in handy to better face it.

There is one more benefit. **The higher your grit in facing your challenges, the more you will inspire your loved ones, friends, and**

others, leaving a lasting legacy. I have no doubt, your courage and positivity, is already touching and will touch many lives.

Please remember that **our goal isn't to force positivity. The happiest people aren't *always* positive.** Instead, they experience authentic emotions. They are happy during happier times and sad when they have a reason to be sad. Nevertheless, they do not sulk and stay in a deep dark place for a very long time.

The program outlined here is adapted from the Stress Management And Resiliency Training (SMART) program that I have developed and tested in over 30 clinical trials.[1-13] Please visit resiliencetrainer.com if you wish to learn more about SMART and our research.

Let me start by sharing a story with you. This is the story of a person whose determination helped him rise in emotional and spiritual resilience, just as his physical body was surrendering to the inevitable. I have thought of him many times as he achieved transformation through disruption. His name was Dylan.

Take care.
Amit

Note: This book is a companion guide to the online course *Resilient Living* at the website resilientliving.net.

Dylan

When I first met Dylan, a thirty-four-year-old gentleman, he looked remarkably healthy for his diagnosis of advanced pancreatic cancer. He was tall, perhaps 6'2", had thick black hair, deeply set brown eyes, and almost a monobrow. If I saw him at the coffee shop, I would have thought he had flown in from out-of-state to discuss his research project with my colleagues. Trish, his wife, sat in the corner,  her eyes staring at the floor, with a crumpled soggy tissue in her right hand. I gave her another tissue.

"I have advanced illness doctor," Dylan said, his eyes scanning the room before they settled on me. "I know what's coming. But I love my life. I love my wife." Dylan brought Trish closer to him. "I want to live the joy of thirty years in one tenth the time. We want to create memories of a lifetime in the time we have. How do we do that?"

I absorbed his words as I readjusted my approach. This wasn't an ordinary stress consult. Dylan was already past the grief, the anger, and the why-me phase. He came straight to the point, was in acceptance, and ready for action. I mustered all my knowledge and experience so I could match his depth.

"I sense your urgency. Every moment is precious. Tell me, what makes you happy, Dylan?"

"Time with Trish, good night's sleep, hot cup of coffee, inspiring stories, music, fixing things around the house. That's for starters."

"What's common in all this?" I asked.

Dylan thought for a moment. "They are the stuff I like to do."

"Yes, and you forget yourself doing them, don't you? You also go deeper into your mind," I said.

Dylan began to say something but then paused. The ticking of the clock filled the moments as Dylan collected his thoughts. It didn't feel awkward.

"But my mind is always going. I try my best to shut it, but it won't quit thinking about the diagnosis. My pancreas sits in every corner of my head. What good will it do to go deeper into the muck?"

Dylan had a point. He had tried his best to "accept" his diagnosis, but acceptance has a limit. Cancer wasn't just a six-letter word for him. It barged in, packed with an abrupt life detour, lost hopes, incomplete stories, the fear of the unknown, not to mention the volleys of pain, nausea, and fatigue.

"You are right, Dylan. The mind can't be shut when it has so many open files. But this I can tell you. The deeper you go, the more peace and stillness you will find, like the quiet in the depth of the ocean on a very stormy night."

Dylan leaned forward and shifted his shoulders toward me. I waited for a few moments, adjusted my glasses, and then continued.

"The drive becomes easier if it has rest areas."

"What do you mean by that?" Dylan asked.

"The rest areas are moments when you are fully present, feeling grateful for the simple things, kind to the self, have hope and courage, and are generous with forgiveness. Even a brief experience of such a pure state can be very healing."

"I have been there occasionally. But only for like, seconds. How do I stay there longer and take Trish with me?"

"Let's explore that together. We will take a back-stage tour of the brain to understand the brain mechanisms that deplete our vitality. I will share a few skills that will help you add those rest areas to your day."

Friend, through this book and the online program, I hope to share with you insights and practices that I shared with Dylan. All of the concepts are built in the form of a daily journal and a structured four-module program so you can learn and apply the ideas in your life at a pace that feels comfortable to you.

It's truly a privilege to walk a few steps with you on this journey.

Editorial Note: A few of the descriptions here are taken from my previous books, *The Resilience Journal,* and *Mindfulness Redesigned.*

Resilient Living

resilientliving.net

How to Use This Book

This book, developed as a journal, invites you to interact with it two to three times a day. Each page of the book has four sections as shown below:

Date: ____ / ____ / _____ Day _____

Insight ➡ **Today's Insight:**
Fear is a common emotion during difficult times, and for good reason. Disabling symptoms, uncertainty about future suffering, loss of preferred lifestyle, worries about leaving others behind, incomplete stories—these concerns and more are woven into the illness and adversity experience. Fear sometimes is helpful, but more often, fear increases our pain.

Fortunately, we can do a lot to optimize our fear. Company of loved ones and friends, having a competent and compassionate caring team, faith, and engagement with positive meaning—all lower our fear. Research shows another simple way to decrease fear and preserve energy is through the practice of gratitude.[1]

Through decreasing fear and enhancing relationships, the practice of gratitude decreases negative mind wanderings, particularly prior to sleep. Research shows that by decreasing these pre-sleep ruminations, gratitude enhances quality of your sleep.[2]

I invite you to spend a few minutes every day practicing gratitude. This would be an excellent investment toward your long-term physical, emotional and spiritual wellbeing, and also your relationships.

Practice ➡

Practice	Set Intention	Assess Action
Morning Gratitude Think about and send silent gratitude to a few people in the morning before you get out of the bed.	☐	☐

Reflection ➡ **Reflection:**
My reflections for today:_____

Quote ➡ *Personal hurts multiply when we visit them too often; personal hurts heal when we tend to others who are hurting.*

Here are three simple steps to use the journal:

Step I: Insight and Set Intention
Try and read the insight for the day. Most insights are research-based inspirations. Underline or highlight the text as you feel appropriate.

Next, set intention for the practice or practices you wish to implement. It is ideal to plan a day ahead (e.g., set intention for the Tuesday practice on Monday evening).

Step II: Practice
Implement the intended practice/s during the day. Note your success in the journal (Assess action).

Step III: Write Your Reflections
Write a few short thoughts—stories, insights, observations, quotes – anything that inspires you and creates positive memories for you and others. You can use the quote for the day as a starter idea.

Every week for the first eight weeks, I will share a specific practice that you can add to your day—as a brief written instruction along with the specific videos at resilientliving.net.

Remember that you don't have to be perfect in any of this. It will be natural for you to forget or not have the desire or energy to do anything some days. That's okay. Further, if a particular skill or idea doesn't resonate with you, then let it go. Choose the practices that make the most sense. Most importantly, be kind to yourself. That's where it all starts.

Our first week starts with a simple two-minute practice—the morning gratitude.

Week 1: Morning Gratitude

Some moments during the day are of outsized importance with respect to our stress and happiness. One time is right when you wake up.

How we wake up

Perhaps a lot of your time is usurped by external demands. But one sacred moment that I suggest you keep as yours is right when you wake up. Often, when I ask people about their first thought when they wake up, it is related to incomplete tasks, the upcoming challenges of the day, or something else similar. For many, the unanswered emails or social media posts draw immediate attention. This is waking up with adrenaline, often thinking about what should I do or dread? **Our ancestors had no choice but to wake up with adrenaline, but we can choose otherwise.**

A suggested alternative

The morning gratitude practice is simple: **Before you get out of the bed, think about a few people in your life who matter a lot to you and send them your silent gratitude for being in your life.**

Instead of describing the whole sequence, I invite you to invest three minutes of your life and practice it with me.

Here is the link to the practice:
https://www.youtube.com/watch?v=0M-TLhGKgwA

It is also available in the accompanying online program.

The advantages of waking up with gratitude include:
- More positive emotions
- Better attention
- Greater intentionality
- Feeling connected to others
- Improved relationships

If you routinely meet someone in the morning, such as your spouse, partner, child, or caregiver—before meeting them, remind yourself why you are grateful to that person. It will change the quality of your connection.

The written steps
Here are the steps. Feel free to have someone read them slowly to you if you wish your loved one or friend to guide you through the practice.

Gently close your eyes and start deep slow smooth breathing.

Think about the first person in your life who matters a lot to you. Recall this person's face. Then send this person a silent gratitude for being in your life.

Second person—get back to the first memory of this person, the first time you saw him or her. Then send your silent gratitude.

Third person—look into the eyes of this person and notice the color of the eyes. Then send your silent gratitude.

Go back in time and look at yourself as an eight-year-old. Recall your hairstyle at that time. Then send a warm hello to your eight-year-old self.

Think of someone who has passed away who you loved. Give that person a virtual hug. And then send silent gratitude to that person.

When you are ready, you may open your eyes.

With time, you are welcome to include people you don't know very well, even those who may have annoyed you in the past, in your gratitude practice.

I highly recommend that you **customize this practice after the initial learning, so it becomes your own.**

If first thing in the morning is tough, you can practice it during the shower. You can add meaning to the practice by assuming that you are protecting the people to whom you are sending your silent gratitude.

In addition, you can practice morning gratitude later during the day, or if you are very busy, only with one or two people if that's all you can accommodate.

The goal is to wake up in control of your attention and feeling grateful instead of grumpy. The practice will lower the adrenaline in your system, help you feel connected and less lonely, experience more uplifting emotions, and develop better attention. All of these benefits can have a profound influence on your health and overall wellbeing.

Please watch the following videos if you are using this journal concurrent with the online program at resilientliving.net:

Module I: Gratitude

Video #	Video Title
1	Introduction
2	The Brain: A Back-stage Tour
3	Focus
4	Fatigue
5	Fear
6	Attention Sumps
7	Putting it all together
8	Morning Gratitude
9	Morning Gratitude: The Practice
10	Morning Gratitude: Creating a Habit

 *Date:* _____ / _____ / _____ *Day* _____

Today's Insight:
Fear is a common emotion during stressful times, and for a good reason. Disabling symptoms, uncertainty about the future, loss of preferred lifestyle, worries about loved ones, sadness about unfulfilled dreams— these concerns and more are woven into any long-term illness and adversity experience. Fear sometimes helps, but very often, fear reflects **F**alse **E**xpectations **A**ppearing **R**eal. The latter fear is unhelpful.

Fortunately, we can do a lot to reduce our fear. Company of loved ones and friends, having a competent and compassionate caring team, faith, and engagement with positive meaning—all lower our fear. Research shows another simple way to decrease fear and preserve energy is through the practice of gratitude.[14] The more grateful you are, the lower your fear.

Further, by decreasing fear and enhancing relationships, gratitude reduces negative mind wanderings, particularly before sleep. Research shows that by decreasing these pre-sleep ruminations, gratitude improves the quality of your sleep.[15]

I invite you to spend a few minutes every day this week practicing gratitude. Gratitude will be an excellent investment toward your long-term physical, emotional and spiritual wellbeing, and also your relationships.

Practice	Set Intention	Assess Action
Morning Gratitude Tomorrow, before I get out of the bed in the morning, I will think about and send silent gratitude to a few people.	☐	☐

Reflection:
My reflections for today:_____

_____

Personal hurts multiply when we visit them too often; personal hurts heal when we tend to others who are hurting.

 *Date*: _____ / _____ / _____ *Day* _____

Today's Insight:
Gratitude can help during good times, and also during struggles. Research shows gratitude enhances the quality of life and decreases psychological distress in people without any illness, in people with early-stage, and even advanced stage condition.[16] This is because authentic gratitude doesn't depend on something big and consequential. You can choose to feel grateful for a cup of pure water, the ability to take a deep breath, the comfort of a warm bed, and the presence of loved ones and friends who care. Interestingly, gratitude for something simple provides the same joy and benefit as gratitude for something more substantial.

Gratitude doesn't mean everything is hunky-dory, so let's celebrate. It means I'll focus on what's right about this moment. I know that tomorrow is uncertain or the past was painful, but for now, I will pick only the load of the next hour since I know that the stronger I am in this moment, the greater the vitality I will have to face the next moment's challenge.

Being blessed is important. It is just as important to be aware of our blessings. Gratitude helps you feel the support you have received, and through that awareness, empowers you to cope better with life's challenges, big or small.[17]

Practice	Set Intention	Assess Action
Morning Gratitude Tomorrow, before I get out of the bed in the morning, I will think about and send silent gratitude to a few people.	☐	☐

Reflection:
My reflections for today:_____

_____

Open your eyes & look up when others want you to shut your eyes and look down. The brightest stars appear on the darkest nights.

Date: _____ / _____ / _____ *Day* _____

Today's Insight:
A few years ago, my then second grader introduced me to the happiest little girl in her school. She was perhaps eight, a recent immigrant. I asked her, "What makes you so happy?" Her response was, "I am happy because the grass is green and soft, the swing sets work, and the sky is so blue." She had come from a place where there was so much smog that she had never seen the blue sky. That day was the first time (despite having celebrated fifty birthdays) that I looked at the blue sky with gratitude.

She reminded me to notice the simple and the ordinary. Notice the grains on the skin of the apple, your pet's eyes, the shape of the clouds, the dew on the grass; hear the birds singing at dawn; smell the fragrance of coffee and feel the warmth of the cup. When immersed in our sensory experience, we push out the default negative thoughts.

The more we realize the preciousness of each day, the more we notice and savor the little details of living.

We eat only a couple of pancakes at breakfast. Why not savor the ones we are eating? No wonder, research shows that being fully present and feeling grateful enhances overall life satisfaction and happiness.[18]

Practice	Set Intention	Assess Action
Morning Gratitude Tomorrow, before I get out of the bed in the morning, I will think about and send silent gratitude to a few people.	☐	☐

Reflection:
My reflections for today:_____

_____

_____

Happier folks don't have more positive & less negative events. They pay more attention to positive & less attention to negative events.

Date: _____ / _____ / _____ *Day* _____

Today's Insight:
During difficult times we often connect with a lot of people such as healthcare professionals, support staff, friends, loved ones, and others. Nevertheless, illness and adversities make us feel lonely. This is true not only for patients but also for their children[19] and caregivers.[20]

Emotional loneliness worsens our physical and emotional health.[21,22] Further, it affects people's ability to focus and remember—essential skills we need during adverse times.[23]

Loneliness has several solutions. Enhancing nurturing social connections and keeping the company of pets helps. Two additional approaches that can decrease loneliness are engagement in meaningful activities and feeling grateful.[24] [25]

Grateful feelings help you become better aware of the connections that already exist. Further, gratitude also helps you make new and deeper connections, including with people you run into every day such as the grocery clerk, elevator operator, security staff, lab technician, nurse, and volunteers. Your gratitude attracts good people in your life. They want to be around you because you embody hope and inspiration. And no one in today's world would mind an extra helping of hope and inspiration.

Practice	Set Intention	Assess Action
Morning Gratitude Tomorrow, before I get out of the bed in the morning, I will think about and send silent gratitude to a few people.	☐	☐

Reflection:
My reflections for today:_____

_____

The joy of remembering a good deed and good people is almost as strong the tenth time as it is the first time.

Date: _____ / _____ / _____ *Day* _____

Today's Insight:
As a child, I remember looking at my reflection in the mirror, noticing and detesting my big nose. I have stopped doing that now but focus more on my receding hairline. We have an instinct to selectively notice what we feel is the least attractive part of us.

When you are unwell or stressed, your body diverts its energy away from self-care to waging war. The resulting strain decreases skin blood flow, causes hair loss, and accelerates aging. Combine that with side effects of the treatments, and in some instances, surgical scars and more—many of us understandably struggle with self-image amidst illness or adversity.[26,27]

Self-care helps as does resilience in protecting your self-image.[28] Two key ingredients of resilience, self-compassion and gratitude are particularly helpful with self-image.[29-31] For example, in one study, people who focused on gratitude had a much better self-image compared to those who focused on hassles.[32] Further, gratitude enhanced self-image not only in patients with illness but also in healthy people and leaders.[33,34]

I have come to realize and accept that every nose is beautiful, even mine! And I'm willing to take my mother's word—a receding hairline is a sign of wisdom.

Practice	Set Intention	Assess Action
Morning Gratitude Tomorrow, before I get out of the bed in the morning, I will think about and send silent gratitude to a few people.	☐	☐

Reflection:
My reflections for today:_____

_____

Humility isn't feeling small or low. Humility is having accurate self-awareness, confidence, and healthy self-worth.

 *Date: _____ / _____ / _____ Day _____*

Today's Insight:
Adverse times are moments when we become more sensitive and feel vulnerable. These are the moments when support from others greatly helps our strength, symptoms, even survival. Unfortunately, these are also the moments when we might not see the love and support that is already there. We also tend to internalize and stew on any perceived insult since we feel physically and emotionally weak.

Several studies show that gratitude can help us appreciate the love and support that already exists. For example, in a study, gratitude enhanced relationship satisfaction among people who felt insecure in their relationships.[35] In another study, gratitude decreased attachment anxiety, helping people feel more secure.[36]

In addition to feeling grateful, expressing gratitude offers additional help. The process of expressing gratitude by itself helps us feel supported.[37]

Feeling and expressing gratitude, thus have an additive effect. Further, the more appreciation you show, the more support comes your way, as I will soon share with you. This would put you in an upward spiral of life—a good place to be.

Practice	Set Intention	Assess Action
Morning Gratitude Tomorrow, before I get out of the bed in the morning, I will think about and send silent gratitude to a few people.	☐	☐

Reflection:
My reflections for today:_____

_____

Just as a honeybee collects nectar from many flowers, collect wisdom & nurturing from many role models, friends, and loved ones.

Date: _____ / _____ / _____ *Day* _____

Today's Insight:
Here is a potpourri of benefits of gratitude:
Expressing gratitude does wonders in building relationships. When you say an authentic thank you, you enhance others' self-worth. With expressing heartfelt gratitude, not only does the receiver of your gratitude feel better connected to you, but you also feel that you have a stronger relationship with that person.[38]

This benefit applies not only within close relationships but also among professionals, including your medical team. Research shows that patients' expression of gratitude improves the performance of the medical team.[39]

Gratitude helps you make better decisions. Research shows when you feel grateful (compared to neutral or angry), you become better in taking advice and judging the accuracy of information.[40]

Gratitude helps you think differently. A good approach amidst adversity is to look for growth opportunities in adverse situations.[41] While we cannot undo the past or custom-design a future to our liking, perhaps we can find a little crack of light through the dark clouds. That may be enough to give us the strength to engage with what is.

Practice	Set Intention	Assess Action
Morning Gratitude Tomorrow, before I get out of the bed in the morning, I will think about and send silent gratitude to a few people.	☐	☐

Reflection:
My reflections for today:_____

_____

Commit to doing something good, however small, each day.
It will be the start of a transformation.

Week 2: Grateful Memories

The morning gratitude practice is one of the many ways you can bring gratitude into your life. You can take grateful notes in a diary, send a text, a handwritten note or an email, or share something more tangible such as a small gift. A simple idea that helps you savor gratitude and build lasting memories is with a gratitude jar.

Gratitude Jar
Take a nice-looking jar and have some scratch paper and a pen handy. Each day think about one good thing that happened or one bad thing that could have happened but didn't.

A good thing could be pain relief, improving blood tests, a good visit with a loved one, friend, or caregiver, your favorite soccer team advanced to the next round (or the less liked team defeated!), or something else.

You can think of countless bad things that could have happened but didn't related to the medical, financial, social, geopolitical, and other aspects of life.

Whenever possible, add humor as you are able. Such as—I am grateful that even though I didn't floss this morning I haven't lost my teeth yet!

Once you have collected a few dozen writings, share the notes at the dining table or another time, create a collage, or capture some of the writings in a New Year's card. Why not play a game—who wrote the funniest (but decent) gratitude thought this week?!

With each of your grateful writings, you are creating a legacy that you and your family will treasure for a very long time.

Please watch the following videos if you are using this journal concurrent with the online program at resilientliving.net:

Module I: Gratitude

Video #	Video Title
11	Gratitude at Work
12	Grateful Memories
13	Module I Summary

 *Date:* _____ / _____ / _____ *Day* _____

Today's Insight:
Gratitude has an interesting effect on relationships. As I shared previously, research shows that gratitude enhances relationship quality.[42] But there is another aspect worth mentioning. Gratitude also increases comfort in voicing relationship concerns.[43] It is thus possible that those who are most grateful to you might be the ones complaining the most!

If you are at the receiving end of a negative feedback, consider one or more of the following perspectives that I try my best to apply when I am feeling unworthy:

Original feeling	A fresh look
Angry with me	Felt close enough to show their raw emotions
Critical of me	Think I am capable of better
Disapproving	Pointing at my past and not the future
Find me unpromising	Challenging me to surprise them
Quick to judge	Perhaps they mean well but don't know better; I will give forgiveness a chance
No matter what: There is more right about me than there is wrong	

Practices	Set Intention	Assess Action
Morning Gratitude	☐	☐
Grateful Memories Note on a scratch paper something simple and good that happened, or something bad that could have happened but didn't.	☐	☐

Reflection:
My reflections for today:_____

_____

> *Even if you are surrounded by the kindest and most well-meaning people, you'll get hurt. Forgiveness is essential to daily happiness.*

Date: _____ / _____ / _____ *Day* _____

Today's Insight:
Here are two examples of how gratitude can help during adverse situations.

Grateful for dirty dishes: On her second birthday, our daughter had to be in the hospital for a significant GI illness. The day she was discharged, I helped her with a bowl of lentil soup. She had declined to eat anything prior. She gulped down the entire bowl. That day I felt grateful for the gift of loading dirty dishes. I shared this thought with my wife: Dirty dishes mean that the family shared a meal together. That perspective has changed the joy I get from loading the dishwasher.

The antidote to emotional poverty: Material poverty has known adverse health consequences, some of which are mediated through changes in genetic expression and inflammation. Interestingly, research shows gratitude can completely neutralize the adverse effect of material poverty on inflammation.[44]

It is true that gratitude may be the last thought coming to our mind during tough times, but maybe that is when gratitude is most needed to preserve our vitality and fill us with positive energy to get through the difficulties.

Practices	Set Intention	Assess Action
Morning Gratitude	☐	☐
Grateful Memories Note on a scratch paper something simple and good that happened, or something bad that could have happened but didn't.	☐	☐

Reflection:
My reflections for today:_____

_____

_____

> *Although we can't change our genetic sequence, we can influence which genes are expressed. And that's a great start.*

Date: _____ / _____ / _____ *Day* _____

Today's Insight:
Helping loved ones live with good values is important to us. We want our children to do the right thing, be respectful, work hard, and treat others with respect and kindness. With the changing world, all of that may not be easy. How do you inspire others to embody the behaviors you wish them to embody? You guessed it right—one idea is to help them feel grateful.

Research shows the kinder you are (and the more people feel grateful toward you), the more likely they emulate your positive behavior.[45] This works both ways—the closer they feel toward you, the more they copy you; the more they copy you, the better your relationship with them, setting up a lovely positive feedback loop.[46]

Another advantage is the company gratitude keeps. The grateful are not only happier and have better relationships, they are also more honest, compared to the less grateful people even if they are equally happy.[47] Gratitude thus is a powerful value that attracts several other positive attributes in our life. The beauty is that despite being so powerful, gratitude is also simple and accessible—a rare combination.

Practices	Set Intention	Assess Action
Morning Gratitude	☐	☐
Grateful Memories Note on a scratch paper something simple and good that happened, or something bad that could have happened but didn't.	☐	☐

Reflection:
My reflections for today:_____

_____

> *People who make us feel unworthy occupy a disproportionate real estate in our head. Cancel their lease, at least for today.*

Date: _____ / _____ / _____ *Day* _____

Today's Insight:
A friend of mine once challenged me at a social event, "How will thinking gratitude or compassion help when I can't get rid of my stressor?" She was drinking tea at that time.

I asked, "What if this tea is very bitter? What will you do?"
"I'll add some sugar to it," she said. "I love my tea."

"It's the same with gratitude and compassion. Adding them to your life may not take the pain away but might dilute the bitterness. The pain as a result becomes less depleting. The energy you save will help you better handle the primary stressor."

Indeed, that's what the research shows. With the reframing and positive emotions, gratitude decreases the symptoms of depression and improves physical health.[48] [49] And the physical changes are measurable in blood tests such as improvement of inflammatory markers in patients with heart disease.[50]

Let the sweet flavors dilute the bitterness and pain in your life.

Practices	Set Intention	Assess Action
Morning Gratitude	☐	☐
Grateful Memories Note on a scratch paper something simple and good that happened, or something bad that could have happened but didn't.	☐	☐

Reflection:
My reflections for today:_____

_____

_____

> *Start your day assuming you are a phenomenal person.*
> *A bad thought, word, or action is unbecoming of you.*

Date: _____ / _____ / _____ *Day* _____

Today's Insight:
Our brain has several discrete areas that host specific predictable functions. Thus, activation of the amygdala evokes negative emotions such as fear, while activation of the reward network correlates with positive feelings. Good news of any type, success in an endeavor, exciting experiences, positive relationships, dark chocolate—they all activate the reward network. Two practices that activate the reward network are compassion and gratitude.[51]

In addition to the reward network, gratitude activates several specific additional areas of the brain (inferior temporal and medial prefrontal cortex).[52] [53]

That's not all. Research shows that the more grateful you feel, the more you are likely to help others.[54,55] You simply have more energy and joy to share with others. The process of helping others by itself activates the reward network of the brain.

No wonder, gratitude and happiness are tightly correlated; the grateful are happier and authentic happiness helps you feel grateful.

Practices	Set Intention	Assess Action
Morning Gratitude	☐	☐
Grateful Memories Note on a scratch paper something simple and good that happened, or something bad that could have happened but didn't.	☐	☐

Reflection:
My reflections for today:_____

_____

How you drive is as important as where you are going.
Perhaps you aren't going anywhere, just becoming a better driver.

Date: _____ / _____ / _____ *Day* _____

Today's Insight:
One feeling that enters the brain's unguarded corner unannounced is envy. Envy inflames the space it resides, activating the pain areas of the brain.[56] The defenders of envy argue that by noticing and comparing, envy helps with motivation. But research doesn't support this notion. The envious, particularly those with the malicious kind of envy are not necessarily more motivated or successful.[57]

Envy originates in the perceived expectation reality mismatch—when we feel we got less than we deserved, while someone else got more than he or she deserved. Even when we get to our satisfaction, if our competitor got more than what we feel he or she deserved, we might feel envious.

How to decrease envy? Focus on their efforts and constraints, not just success. Consider gratitude. Research shows gratitude enhances the mild inspiring form of envy while it blunts the malicious hurtful envy.[58]

The lower your envy, the fewer your interpersonal conflicts. Conflicts drain energy. Conflict avoidance is particularly important during stressful times, to preserve your energy for health and healing.[59]

Practices	Set Intention	Assess Action
Morning Gratitude	☐	☐
Grateful Memories Note on a scratch paper something simple and good that happened, or something bad that could have happened but didn't.	☐	☐

Reflection:
My reflections for today:_____

_____

Birds with asymmetric feathers are the ones that can fly. Symmetry looks pretty, but sometimes life's asymmetries help us ascend.

Date: _____ / _____ / _____ *Day* _____

Today's Insight:
I hope in the previous two weeks you added a little extra gratitude flavor to your life. As you can see and is proven in research, gratitude helps almost every single aspect of our life. This is true irrespective of age.[60] And by lowering your threshold to feel grateful, you need to do nothing else but appreciate what you already have to experience positive emotions.

One aspect we haven't covered yet is gratitude among healthcare providers. Of late, research is highlighting that partly because of the rapid invasion of technology, healthcare providers are experiencing much more stress and burnout. When they receive grateful expressions from others, their stress goes down, and professional satisfaction improves. This is particularly true when they are having a difficult day.[61]

So, consider including your healthcare providers in your gratitude practice. Consider writing something positive about them and placing it in your gratitude jar. And if you feel it is appropriate, let them know you appreciate the care you have received. Authentic appreciation enhances the quality of care you and your loved ones receive.

Practices	Set Intention	Assess Action
Morning Gratitude	☐	☐
Grateful Memories Note on a scratch paper something simple and good that happened, or something bad that could have happened but didn't.	☐	☐

Reflection:
My reflections for today:_____

_____

_____

Technology that doesn't deepen relationships and kindness often hurts us in the long term. Every entrepreneur's brain needs a heart.

Week 3: Curious Moments

Curiosity is the love of learning. Thank heavens for the curiosity of our little ones! Their curiosity helps them learn the most important details there are to know—to survive and succeed on this planet. But as we celebrate more birthdays, our curiosity fades. We start experiencing the world with our ingrained biases that slow our learning and growth. The reasons are many: screen overload, a heavy load of open files, relationship issues, and more.

The curious moments practice is designed to help overcome the attention attrition that happens these days to many of us. The practice might also keep your brain young.

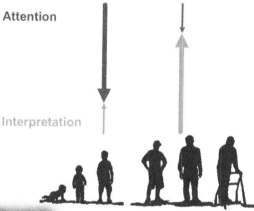

Here is how it works: Your every experience has two key ingredients: **attention and interpretations.** As we get older and the world becomes familiar, interpretations dominate our experience. This change decreases noticing and feeling. It increases the time

we are in our head. **The curious moments practice helps you fill your moments with greater Attention and fewer Interpretations (Increasing the AI ratio).**

As an example, notice this daisy. For a moment, let its image completely take over your mind.

You will notice the multiple layers of petals, lines on the surface, jagged edges of the petals, the dark spot in the center, the stalk at two o'clock position.

With this noticing, you aren't looking at any daisy. You are **getting to know *this* daisy**, in all its uniqueness.

Continuing on the theme, notice three details in the image of the ballerinas—their respective hand positions, their leg alignment, and where they are looking.

With practice, you start using your eyes as a camera, savoring the details in the world around you with deeper attention. These practices are very useful for children to help preserve their attention, failing which they get lost in the gadgets.

Try to notice at least one new detail every day and record it in your journal.

If you wish, you can partner with someone, sharing the novelty you both noticed during the day. Partnering with children, encouraging them to notice one new detail at school and then letting them describe it, might not only provide a good starter topic for evening conversation but also preserve their attention.

An interesting observation is that just as novelty catches your attention, when you choose to pay attention, you start finding more novelty. That's an interesting way to get out of our heads and train our minds to not come in the way of nurturing sensory perceptions.

Please watch the following videos if you are using this journal concurrent with the online program at resilientliving.net:

Module II: Mindful Presence

Video #	Video Title
14	What is Mindful Presence?
15	Your Three Domains of Attention
16	Curious Moments: The Basis
17	Curious Moments: The Practice
18	Curious Living

Date: _____ / _____ / _____ *Day* _____

Today's Insight:
Our brain likes new and novel experiences and dreads boredom. In a study, men would rather give themselves painful electric shocks than sit alone and get bored.[62] Boredom, however, is unavoidable. Very likely, you live in the same house with the same people and drive on the same roads, month after month. How does one find novelty?

Knowledge gap: A simple idea is to create a small knowledge gap in your mind. Here is how to do it. Try to know a little extra about something. Such as, how do the researchers create new varieties of apples? Or, when was the clinic or hospital you recently visited established? Pick one medication you are taking and find out which drug company developed it first and who were the scientists involved? Or perhaps, what does Wikipedia say about the story of your town?

Once you know a little, you might long to know a bit more, sometimes a lot more. None of this might provide any tangible benefit. That's precisely how curiosity works—curiosity for the sake of curiosity.[63] A few curious weeks will make you happier and much better informed about your world.

Practices	Set Intention	Assess Action
Morning Gratitude	☐	☐
Grateful Memories	☐	☐
Curious Moments I'll notice at least one new thing or one new detail in a familiar thing.	☐	☐

Reflection:
My reflections for today:_____

_____

> *The quality of your attention has greater effect on the quality of your experience than the details of your task.*

Date: _____ / _____ / _____ Day _____

Today's Insight:
Within reason, most people appreciate your interest in what they do or who they are. No wonder, curiosity helps you build deeper relationships.[64]

Small bets: A simple trick I often use while waiting for an elevator is to make a bet with someone standing by my side—which elevator will come next, one on the left or the right? Waiting for the elevator then becomes play. We often walk away with a laugh and feeling good about each other.

During travels: At the airport, notice how many people are wearing a hat and what kind. While driving, I often play a game with my family—how many yellow and orange cars (minus the cabs) we will notice. Or how many cars that are the same make, model, and color as ours we will see. It makes the ride a little more interesting.

Your curiosity about the simple often leads to a higher order curiosity. At its least, it might help you be more informed. With time, you might acquire more knowledge about the world and develop the most precious attribute—greater wisdom.

Practices	Set Intention	Assess Action
Morning Gratitude	☐	☐
Grateful Memories	☐	☐
Curious Moments I'll notice at least one new thing or one new detail in a familiar thing.	☐	☐

Reflection:
My reflections for today:_____

_____

_____

When you are not flying the plane, let your brain rest in the airplane mode.

Date: _____ / _____ / _____ *Day* _____

Today's Insight:
Curiosity, by engaging your brain with the world around you, enhances learning and memory.[65] This is particularly true for the seniors who may have fewer memory reserves compared to the young adults.[66] [67]

Your state's license plate: A simple curiosity practice is to get to know your state's license plate. Find one detail in your state's license plate you hadn't noticed before. For example, the Minnesota license plate has a canoe in it with two people sitting in the canoe. You can look at the license plate of different states and compare which ones have the images of nature, are celebrating their favorite sports team, or have some other message!

Your unique hands: Notice which finger is longer in your hands—pointer or ring? Are your hands symmetric or is the pointer finger longer on one hand while the ring finger is on the other? How does it compare with your loved ones and friends? While this might seem like a silly little detail, perhaps it will open your mind to the idea of noticing more prominent details that are right in front of you, but you may be failing to see.

Practices	Set Intention	Assess Action
Morning Gratitude	☐	☐
Grateful Memories	☐	☐
Curious Moments I'll notice at least one new thing or one new detail in a familiar thing.	☐	☐

Reflection:
My reflections for today:_____

_____

_____

If the moon appeared only once a year, we will be awake all night watching it. Savor the beauty of the moon tonight with this thought.

Date: _____ / _____ / _____ *Day* _____

Today's Insight:
Most activities I suggest in our journey together are likely to have one thing in common—they activate the brain's reward network. Curiosity is one of them.[68,69]

A tree close to you: Look at a tree in your neighborhood. Study its branching pattern in all the intricate details. Pick a leaf of the tree and notice the elaborately detailed veins on its surface. You will be amazed that almost every little thing around you has interesting details carved on it. If you wish, draw a portrait of the tree true to how it is branching. Instead of a tree you can pick something else if you wish.

Do you have your newborn handprints or footprints saved somewhere? How about the prints of your children, spouse, siblings, or grandkids?

Curiosity begets curiosity. When you choose to find novelty in your world, you exercise and strengthen the brain's curiosity muscle. An interesting fact is that just as novelty draws greater attention, when you choose to pay attention, you start finding novelty (I know I am repeating myself here!).

Practices	Set Intention	Assess Action
Morning Gratitude	☐	☐
Grateful Memories	☐	☐
Curious Moments I'll notice at least one new thing or one new detail in a familiar thing.	☐	☐

Reflection:
My reflections for today:_____

_____

_____

Each undone task takes double the headspace compared to a completed task or one for which you have a plan.

Date: _____ / _____ / _____ *Day* _____

Today's Insight:
Curiosity helps you expand the repertoire of what is.[70] Cultivating curiosity enables you to re-live the joy of being a child.

Revisit youth: In a 1979 study (called the "counterclockwise" study), when senior men lived as if it was 1959, their biology shifted to a more youthful state. Consider watching a movie on an old VHS tape that you enjoyed when you were a ten-year-old. Play board games you did as a child. Look up your place of birth, your kindergarten school, and where you first dated on Google Earth. If possible, visit one of these places.

Everything is alive: As a child, my handwriting was terrible. I used to dig my pen into the paper. My teacher taught a clever lesson. He said, "Write as if the paper is alive. Do not dig lest you might hurt the paper." That simple instruction helped me become a more mindful and kindful writer.

For a few hours, be gentle and kind to everything around you. Close the door gently, iron your clothes with fuller presence, savor your meal, be 'present' in your shower, write in neat handwriting, and more. It will add extra joy to your day.

Practices	Set Intention	Assess Action
Morning Gratitude	☐	☐
Grateful Memories	☐	☐
Curious Moments I'll notice at least one new thing or one new detail in a familiar thing.	☐	☐

Reflection:
My reflections for today:_____

_____

We aren't physical beings having a physical experience.
We are spiritual beings having a spiritual experience.

 *Date:* _____ / _____ / _____ *Day* _____

Today's Insight:
When you are experiencing significant adversity, the busiest organ of your body is the brain. It is continually thinking and planning for all the what-ifs. The brain networks that host planning and problem-solving overheat, which decreases their effectiveness. They need some rest to function well again. Curiosity can provide that respite.

Research shows that curiosity enhances coping when going through significant adversity.[71] Experiences that shift your attention from inward focus toward the outer world can help. Thus, patients with depression improve faster in sunny hospital rooms that pull their attention outward.[72]

Try this: Give a pause to planning or problem solving and enjoy an activity such as singing along with an old song or writing with your non-dominant hand. Consider rhyming or writing poetry.

In a store or on the internet, study the logos of your favorite brand (text, color, shape, overall design). Research the history of one or more of the logos. You might discover details that fascinate you.

Practices	Set Intention	Assess Action
Morning Gratitude	☐	☐
Grateful Memories	☐	☐
Curious Moments I'll notice at least one new thing or one new detail in a familiar thing.	☐	☐

Reflection:
My reflections for today:_____

_____

_____

The fear of vulnerability weakens us worse than the vulnerability itself. Your weakness becomes strength when you let go of the fear.

Date: _____ / _____ / _____ *Day* _____

Today's Insight:
Curiosity not only helps you be happier, build relationships, and have better memory and learning, but also might increase your longevity. The health benefits of curiosity are particularly relevant for senior people.[73]

Discover brilliance: Ask people what they are good at and invite them to share their expertise. I have met expert self-trained expert carpenters, weathermen, builders, computer geeks, chefs, farmers, and more.

This beautiful world: Curiosity helps you acquire information and better understand the world. Pick up a book on cosmology or watch a few videos on the NASA's YouTube channel to learn about our universe.

An alternative world: Consider learning a bit about palmistry, astrology, or another such skill. While you may agree or disagree with astrology, it will open you to a fascinating new world visited by millions of people.

Share a part of you: Write five top inspiring stories from your life and share them with others. If you wish, share those stories with me by emailing me at as@resilientoption.com. I will try my best to respond.

Practices	Set Intention	Assess Action
Morning Gratitude	☐	☐
Grateful Memories	☐	☐
Curious Moments I'll notice at least one new thing or one new detail in a familiar thing.	☐	☐

Reflection:
My reflections for today:_____

_____

Being tough doesn't mean becoming callous and uncaring.
It means letting yourself cry and finding a smile as the tears dry.

Week 4: The Two-Minute Rule

Research shows we pay attention to the people closest to us for only 90-seconds before we get busy with our gadgets or other "more important" things.

The result is that we lose the next generation to the feast of information they are receiving from the internet. **Having Smartphone (even when switched off) at the dining table is enough to hurt the quality of conversation.** The two-minute rule practice invites you to invest at least two minutes of committed time to connect authentically with someone.

Let's do a thought experiment. You are sitting with your spouse or partner in a cafeteria, and your high school buddy shows up who you haven't met for twenty years. Who will be more interesting for the next two minutes—your spouse/partner or your highschool buddy? Almost everyone says it is the highschool buddy. The reason for that is novelty.

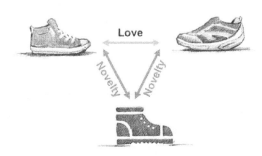

The key to engaged presence is finding novelty where love is. What does that look like?

Imagine you haven't met your family for a month. Will you find them a little more interesting when you meet them after that long a gap? Most people agree with that assumption. Here is how I leveraged this idea into a practice I have been doing for the last ten years.

The practice
Before getting into home at the end of the day, I started reminding myself, "I am going to meet some very special people who I haven't met for a month." With that intention, I would go inside. Every day became better.

When that didn't work, I started reminding myself: My ten-year-old will be off to college in about 2500 days. This awareness gave me a perspective and permission to leave my work-related ruminations in the background.

Here are the two components of the two-minute rule practice:

Find them novel and meaningful: **Assume that your loved ones are novel and meaningful every day, more than you can imagine.** A simple way to engage is to make it a habit to look at the color of their eyes (only for two seconds) within 30 seconds of entering the home. Why 30 seconds? Because most of our connection happens in that much time. Miss the first 30 seconds, and you might have missed the entire evening. Also, try to say something that helps them know that they were in your thoughts (in a good way) when you were away from them. Another option is to tell them how they were right about something!

Do not try to improve right away: A (mostly unhelpful) instinct we have is to improve others the moment we see them. When we do that, they start associating us with feeling bad about themselves. So, as a part of the two-minute rule practice, **do not try to improve anyone for the first two minutes you are with them.**

Expanding the practice
These skills are not limited to happy families. They apply just as much to your friends, neighbors, colleagues, and clients.

They also apply to pets, dogs in particular. Dogs are master practitioners of the two-minute rule practice.

A perfect way to practice the two-minute rule practice is to keep the context in mind when meeting someone outside of your home or immediate workplace, such as at the grocery store. You have to do nothing else but to remember that the person in front of you has a bigger universe in which he or she is very precious. Such an assumption and remembrance will enhance your experience with that person.

The key is to do your best to show you are in a good mood, in a predictable fashion.

I suggest you tweak these ideas, so they fit well in your personal life. For example, if you live alone, then you can practice this with your pet, a close friend, perhaps even a kind neighbor or a colleague. The idea is to **meet at least one person during the day with authentic, non-judgmental presence.** Such presence is very healing and uplifting for both you and the person receiving your authentic attention.

Also, no need to push yourself on days you don't have dispensable energy. Being kind to yourself is as important as being kind to others. Next week, we will spend much more time with kindness.

Please watch the following videos if you are using this journal concurrent with the online program at resilientliving.net. You'll notice that the first practice is Scheduled Worry Time. It is geared to preventing worries from taking over your entire day. Try it if it makes sense to you after watching the video.

Module II: Mindful Presence

Video #	Video Title
19	Scheduled Worry Time
20	The Two-Minute Rule
21	Expanding the Two-Minute Rule
22	Module II Summary

Date: _____ / _____ / _____ *Day* _____

Today's Insight:
Interesting research shows that while finding novelty can enhance happiness, the greatest joy is in pursuits that have social aspects.[74] This is because one of the most potent sources of our happiness is relationships.

One challenge in connecting with people is that we sometimes get overwhelmed by the differences and at the same time get bored by the familiar. Here are two solutions:

- When you meet new people, try to find familiarity with them. Do they have similar concerns as you, shared dreams, have visited similar places, and more?
- When you are with the familiar people, try to find novelty about them. Have they visited a new place recently, read something interesting, tried a new book, met someone you don't know?

A good way to enjoy connections with others is to find familiar in the novel and the novel in the familiar.

Practices	Set Intention	Assess Action
Morning Gratitude	☐	☐
Grateful Memories	☐	☐
Curious Moments	☐	☐
The Two-Minute Rule I'll meet at least one person for two minutes as if I haven't seen him or her for a month. I'll choose not to improve anyone in that time.	☐	☐

Reflection:
My reflections for today:_____

_____

Empty the space in your brain that is usurped by self-doubt.
Replace it with hope, inspiration, and courage.

Date: _____ / _____ / _____ *Day* _____

Today's Insight:
Human thought is often about unfulfilled tasks, concerns, regrets, hurts, and more. While you cannot altogether remove these unhelpful mind wanderings, taking back control of the attention at least a few times a day and directing it toward more nurturing thoughts can be helpful. Specifically, at least once during the day think of the people who care about you. Such thoughts by themselves will enhance your happiness.[75]

Adverse times bring us in contact with many new people in our community who help us overcome the crisis. A simple way to nurture deeper connection with others is to see them in their circle of love. The more you see others, knowing they are special and precious, the better your engagement with them, and the more worthy they feel in your presence. The more worthy they feel, the better their ability to help you.

Thus, thinking about the people close to you and seeing others in their circle of love is an excellent way to feel good and be better served.

Practices	Set Intention	Assess Action
Morning Gratitude	☐	☐
Grateful Memories	☐	☐
Curious Moments	☐	☐
The Two-Minute Rule I'll meet at least one person for two minutes as if I haven't seen him or her for a month. I'll choose not to improve anyone in that time.	☐	☐

Reflection:
My reflections for today:_____

_____

_____

If the world gets cold on you, you'll have to get tough and thick-skinned like the evergreens to survive the winter.

Date: _____ / _____ / _____ *Day* _____

Today's Insight:
I am sure you have heard or read about inflammation. It is our body's response to repair an injury. When exaggerated, the same response can hurt us by clogging our arteries, promoting cancer growth, and damaging the organs. Researchers are looking at newer drugs to control inflammation. A simple strategy is to develop better relationships.

Research shows that the more connected we feel with others, the lower the level of our inflammatory markers.[76] This is true across populations and types of support.

Interestingly, connection with others, beyond our loved ones can also help. Better connections with the neighbors can improve health conditions caused by inflammation. In several research studies having better connections with our neighbors was associated with a lowered risk of stroke and heart attack by 15 to 20%.[77-79] Today might be a great day to thank your good neighbors, for helping you in so many different ways!

Practices	Set Intention	Assess Action
Morning Gratitude	☐	☐
Grateful Memories	☐	☐
Curious Moments	☐	☐
The Two-Minute Rule I'll meet at least one person for two minutes as if I haven't seen him or her for a month. I'll choose not to improve anyone in that time.	☐	☐

Reflection:
My reflections for today:_____

_____

_____

In this world of infinite personalities and agendas, some people are bound to be allergic to you. Focus on the other eight billion.

Today's Insight:

My mother always says one plus one equals eleven and not two. The more research I review about the value of connections, the more convinced I get about their power. Here are two additional lines of studies:

- Quality connections improve blood sugar and clinical outcomes in people with diabetes.[80]
- Having strong personal connections lowers risk factors for heart attack, and in people with heart disease, enhances the chances of survival.[81]

Just as the trail is slightly different each day you walk on it, your loved ones and friends are fresh and new each day. Interesting research shows that similar to how an attractive face draws our attention, when you start paying attention to any face, it starts looking more attractive.[82]

Thus, invest your moments in meaningful connections—to be healthier, happier, and live longer.

Practices	Set Intention	Assess Action
Morning Gratitude	☐	☐
Grateful Memories	☐	☐
Curious Moments	☐	☐
The Two-Minute Rule I'll meet at least one person for two minutes as if I haven't seen him or her for a month. I'll choose not to improve anyone in that time.	☐	☐

Reflection:

My reflections for today:_____

_____

One of the best ways to be liked by others
is to let them know that you like them.

Date: _____ / _____ / _____ *Day* _____

Today's Insight:

Does anyone you know struggle with being appreciated too much? It is fair to assume that every person you meet has struggled with low self-worth. You can help others and yourself by helping them generate positive experiences (researchers believe that to feel good, we need three to five positive experiences for each negative experience).[83] Here are three ideas:

Share: Share details (as appropriate) about you. When you share with others, they feel they are part of your inner circle.[84] Keeping everything to yourself could feel burdensome[85] and increases risk of depression.[86] Some details, however, may not feel right to share with family and friends. Consider sharing with your therapist or coach, as you feel appropriate.

Listen: Listen with full presence because your authentic listening activates others' reward network, a key area of the brain that hosts happiness.[87]

Discover: Find the child in a grownup, and a grownup in a child. This discovery process will connect you with them and help them feel worthy.

Practices	Set Intention	Assess Action
Morning Gratitude	☐	☐
Grateful Memories	☐	☐
Curious Moments	☐	☐
The Two-Minute Rule I'll meet at least one person for two minutes as if I haven't seen him or her for a month. I'll choose not to improve anyone in that time.	☐	☐

Reflection:

My reflections for today:_____

_____

The good people are very good at feeling bad about themselves. If you've felt bad about yourself, it's proof that you're a good person.

Date: _____ / _____ / _____ *Day* _____

Today's Insight:
Here is relationship 101: It is tough to dislike someone who you know likes you. Countless times I have helped my patients and others improve their relationships with loved ones and friends using this simple idea—shower authentic praise on others.

A deserving praise not shared is like a gift packed but never given. Most people do not regret the love they expressed or received. They regret the love they felt but didn't communicate; the love they sought but never got.

The reality is most people feel alone, anxious, and struggle with self-worth. Why not connect with one person today to help him or her feel accepted, happier, and worthy? Remind others of the meaning they are fulfilling, of what they mean to you. Try to remember their small preferences, pay undivided attention, shower authentic praise, share a personally important memorable object with them, pray for them. Each of these and more will bring a smile to their face, and to yours.

Practices	Set Intention	Assess Action
Morning Gratitude	☐	☐
Grateful Memories	☐	☐
Curious Moments	☐	☐
The Two-Minute Rule I'll meet at least one person for two minutes as if I haven't seen him or her for a month. I'll choose not to improve anyone in that time.	☐	☐

Reflection:
My reflections for today:_____

_____

Allow only those things to bother you that will continue to bother you in five years. Look at the truth in its most optimistic version.

Today's Insight:

We touch others with our words and actions. Our well-meaning physical touch is also helpful and healing. Here is some research on physical touch:

* Touch may be more powerful than words in expressing emotions.[88]
* Four out of five patients value touch to feel empathy and connection.[89]
* Distal touch (hands and shoulders) is comforting, particularly when someone familiar touches you.[90]
* Touch between intimate partners enhances bonding and wellbeing.[91]
* Kind touch improves several biological markers.[92]
* Holding hands prior to public speaking lowers blood pressure.[93]
* Slow affective touch decreases pain and feelings of social exclusion.[94]
* Touch can convey eight different feelings—anger, fear, disgust, love, gratitude, sympathy, happiness, and sadness.[95]
* NBA players' early-season touch predicts late-season success.[96]

Use some of these findings to your benefit.[97] Also know that holding something warm in your hands feels similar to holding a loved one's hand (similar, but not the same!).[98]

Practices	Set Intention	Assess Action
Morning Gratitude	☐	☐
Grateful Memories	☐	☐
Curious Moments	☐	☐
The Two-Minute Rule I'll meet at least one person for two minutes as if I haven't seen him or her for a month. I'll choose not to improve anyone in that time.	☐	☐

Reflection:
My reflections for today:_____

_____

Hurry decimates quality and joy. Avoid time pressure by keeping your to-do list short & your not-to-do list long (as much as feasible).

Week 5: Kind Attention

For most of us, the richest source of our sensory input is our eyes. However, we seldom think about how we use our eyes, especially how we look at each other. Allow me to share why that is important.

Let's say you are doing a barbecue in the backyard. You hear some sounds and see the gentleman on the left charging at your home. Are you going to spread the red carpet and say: "Welcome have my dinner?" Or, will you call for help? The answer is obvious.

Our ancestors had to survive these occurrences fairly frequently. People stole each other's cattle, burned homes, and more. And they didn't have 911. They had to fend for themselves. To survive, the first instinct our ancestors needed was suspicion. That instinct has continued.

Look at the person to the right for a brief second. Research shows in less than half a second, most of us will have made judgments about trustworthiness, competence, aggressiveness, attractiveness, and the likeability of this person.

Trustworthiness
Competence
Aggressiveness
Attractiveness
Likeability

Because of this instinct, **when you go to a mall, a dozen people judge you within a few seconds.** Most of these judgments are superficial and unhelpful.

A much better way of looking at each other is with kind attention.

Kind attention: Kind attention recognizes the following two truths –
Special: **This person in front of me is special.** For someone, perhaps many, this person is priceless.
Struggling: **This person in front of me has struggles,** just as I and we all do. Likely, this person's struggles are different than mine, but struggles they are nonetheless.

With that awareness, you have a choice: **when looking at another person, let your instincts judge that person or send him or her a silent "I wish you well."**

Remember that the practice is silent. It is just an intention. Speaking it aloud might feel a little cultish. Also, best not to try kind attention in a dark elevator at 2 AM. Consider using the kind attention practice at family events, in the hospital, at the workplace, past airport security check, at parent-teacher meetings, and wherever you feel comfortable and safe.

Wishing well walk: A simple way to practice kind attention, if your physical health allows, is to take out five-minutes during the day and walk at home or at your workplace and during that time send a silent good wish to everyone you see. This is an easy and an effective way to experience uplifting emotions and pull energy out of thin air. Kind attention is also an effortless way to push away loneliness and lift your self-worth.

You can enhance this practice by becoming creative about how you apply kindness. A few ideas I have tried that have worked for me are:
- ◊ When flying above a city, I often send kind attention to every citizen living there
- ◊ When I see an airliner in the sky, I send positive thoughts to everyone sitting inside and wish them safe travels
- ◊ When passing a pharmacy aisle, I send good wishes to everyone who would be coming there today for medications to relieve their symptoms
- ◊ When opening a doorknob, I often send warm feelings to everyone who held or will hold that doorknob today

◊ Before sleeping at night, sometimes I send healing thoughts to every parent who can't sleep tonight because they are tending to a sick child.

I will revisit some of these (and additional) ideas in the daily practice.

Remember this simple truth: **when you wish someone well, you wish two people well—one is the other person and who is the second person? Yourself!**

Please watch the following videos if you are using this journal concurrent with the online program at resilientliving.net.

Module III: Kindness

Video #	Video Title
23	The Kindness Mortar
24	Why is Kindness Fading?
25	Kind Attention: The Basis
26	Kind Attention: The Practice
27	Creative with Kindness
28	Self-Kindness
29	Self-Kindness: Few Extra Smiles

 *Date*: _____ / _____ / _____ *Day* _____

Today's Insight:
An interesting fact about your brain is that imagination and tangible experience both activate the same part of the brain. Thus, guided imagery gets you relaxed, nightmares get you anxious, constructive daydreaming helps you feel hopeful, and thinking about someone else's pain activates your pain network. You can leverage this insight to experience positivity in your life.

Here are two imaginations that can help bring you extra positivity:
Virtual hugs: Hugs help your heart connect with others'. Close your eyes and think about someone who matters a lot to you. Imagine being in the presence of that person and give that person a virtual hug.

Previous kind actions: Think about a previous kind action of yours and try to remember it in all its vivid details.

Practices	Set Intention	Assess Action
Morning Gratitude	☐	☐
Grateful Memories	☐	☐
Curious Moments	☐	☐
The Two-Minute Rule	☐	☐
Kind Attention I'll assume that most people I meet are special and struggling. I'll send a silent good wish to as many as I can.	☐	☐

Reflection:
My reflections for today:_____

_____

When you get busy helping the world, the world gets busy helping you. The world, however, is almost always slower than desirable.

Date: _____ / _____ / _____ *Day* _____

Today's Insight:
Once I was feeling poorly, alone in my hospital bed. I was too tired to watch TV or read anything. Then, as I looked at the bed and the blanket, I thought of others who may have used the bed before me. I also thought of those who will be using the bed after me. Many would have more struggles than I did. I sent all of them my kind wishes. Not only did I feel connected with many, my feelings and energy both improved.[99]

We connect with others only for a short time. Our constant companion is our mind. Send kindness to the people who are separated from you by space and time. By creatively thinking kind thoughts all day long, you give your mind small snacks of positivity that don't depend on anyone.

Create your own creative ideas of how you will be kind today. With time, you won't be an occasional visitor to the planet of kindness; you will build it within your own mind and thrive in it.

Practices	Set Intention	Assess Action
Morning Gratitude	☐	☐
Grateful Memories	☐	☐
Curious Moments	☐	☐
The Two-Minute Rule	☐	☐
Kind Attention I'll assume that most people I meet are special and struggling. I'll send a silent good wish to as many as I can.	☐	☐

Reflection:
My reflections for today:_____

_____

Hope doesn't mean it won't ever get dark. Hope means no matter how dark the night, the sun will always appear in the morning.

Date: _____ / _____ / _____ *Day* _____

Today's Insight:
I believe the universe protects the protector. The more you think of helping others, the more your brain says, "I am needed in this world." Your body's physiology starts changing—your immune system improves, your genetic expression changes, your inflammation is tamed.[100,101]

A simple way to get all these benefits is to think of how you can help someone who is struggling. It could be someone struggling with self-worth, finances, an old hurt, or something else. You can help others by offering words that help them feel validated. Additionally, if the situation warrants and you are able, you can do something more tangible.

Show extra respect to people who remain invisible such as the hospital janitor, the housekeeping staff at a hotel, or the luggage handler at the baggage claim. Showing gratitude for their work and sharing authentic praise will help them feel worthy and also enhance your self-worth.

Practices	Set Intention	Assess Action
Morning Gratitude	☐	☐
Grateful Memories	☐	☐
Curious Moments	☐	☐
The Two-Minute Rule	☐	☐
Kind Attention I'll assume that most people I meet are special and struggling. I'll send a silent good wish to as many as I can.	☐	☐

Reflection:
My reflections for today:_____

_____

The dollars you earn isn't a barometer of your success. Your success is in the values you embody and the purpose you serve.

Today's Insight:
Most parents would gladly take their children's pain on themselves. Often, when faced with a serious illness, people think less about what will happen to them and more about how they can make sure others, particularly the young others, can carry on with minimal disruption.

Tending to the young ones is our instinct. Several decades ago, on a hot New Delhi afternoon, as my wife and I were eating an ice-cream, we saw a little child looking at us. He seemed hungry. The ice-cream cup we bought for him has nourished us more than any. If you can, do something little for a child. It will lift your day.

Kindness is easiest toward children, particularly those children who we know are struggling. A very simple kindness practice is to think about and send good wishes to all the children in the world who are being rushed to the hospital today for emergency care. Thinking about and sending good wishes to others who are struggling decreases our own pain.

Practices	Set Intention	Assess Action
Morning Gratitude	☐	☐
Grateful Memories	☐	☐
Curious Moments	☐	☐
The Two-Minute Rule	☐	☐
Kind Attention I'll assume that most people I meet are special and struggling. I'll send a silent good wish to as many as I can.	☐	☐

Reflection:
My reflections for today:_____

_____

Fill your past with gratitude not regrets, present with meaning not greed, and future with hope not fear.

Date: _____ / _____ / _____ *Day* _____

Today's Insight:
One of the simplest and most powerful ways to develop compassion is to find commonalities. Here are some of my personal experiences and preferences. Check which of the following apply to you:

Been to Canada	☐	Love chocolate	☐
Behind on sleep	☐	Want to plant more trees	☐
Concerned about the children	☐	Not disciplined about flossing	☐
Love pets	☐	Prefer paper over plastic	☐

As we go down the list and find more commonalities between us, you and I get better connected, and more compassionate to one another.[102,103] Leverage this instinct by finding commonalities with others. Your compassion protects you from depression,[104] and helps you recover faster.[105]

Practices	Set Intention	Assess Action
Morning Gratitude	☐	☐
Grateful Memories	☐	☐
Curious Moments	☐	☐
The Two-Minute Rule	☐	☐
Kind Attention I'll assume that most people I meet are special and struggling. I'll send a silent good wish to as many as I can.	☐	☐

Reflection:
My reflections for today:_____

_____

_____

I have never met a compassionate person who lacked competence. When we preserve compassion, we preserve it all.

Today's Insight:
An authentic smile, the one where your eyes are also smiling, not just your lips, not only helps you feel better physically, it also enhances the quality of care you receive.[106,107] You validate others when you smile at them; your smile helps them feel worthy. Research shows that people are willing to give up money in exchange for receiving an authentic smile.[108] Your joyful feelings project deeper within. They lower your adrenaline, relax your heart, change gene expression, and increase your resilience.

Try adding a few extra smiles to your day during these three moments:
Say hello with a smile: Smile the moment you say hello on the phone to the person on the other side (even to a telemarketer!).
Smile at your reflection: Instead of focusing on some perceived imperfection, smile at yourself in the mirror.
When opening your Smartphone: If you open your Smartphone with face scan, then smile at that moment instead of adopting a neutral look.

Practices	Set Intention	Assess Action
Morning Gratitude	☐	☐
Grateful Memories	☐	☐
Curious Moments	☐	☐
The Two-Minute Rule	☐	☐
Kind Attention I'll assume that most people I meet are special and struggling. I'll send a silent good wish to as many as I can.	☐	☐

Reflection:
My reflections for today:_____

_____

_____

> *Never let someone who shouldn't be in the*
> *story of your life write the title of the story.*

 *Date*: _____ / _____ / _____ *Day* _____

Today's Insight:
The world has more struggles than our individual ability to cope or reframe. Focusing on all the global hurts will increase your pain, decrease hope and worsen your mood.[109-111] Just as the earth supports life by holding its atmosphere in the vacuum of space, hold on to your positivity to preserve your vitality. Hope is even more important when hope is difficult to come by.

If you wish to grow your compassion, instead of focusing on the world's suffering, think of someone mildly annoying or someone you may have blamed in the past.[112,113] Bringing in compassion for such a person will help free your mind from the negativity that person brought into your life.

A simple practice is to pray for someone who angered you.[114] For people who have an anchor of faith, prayer for the loved ones, as well as the annoying ones, is a meaningful act of compassion and healing.

Practices	Set Intention	Assess Action
Morning Gratitude	☐	☐
Grateful Memories	☐	☐
Curious Moments	☐	☐
The Two-Minute Rule	☐	☐
Kind Attention I'll assume that most people I meet are special and struggling. I'll send a silent good wish to as many as I can.	☐	☐

Reflection:
My reflections for today:_____

_____

_____

Forgiveness takes the power from the other person and empowers you to choose your mindset based on your values.

Week 6: Kind Meditation

We are a meaning-seeking species. A practice or an activity has to be either enjoyable (e.g., eating an ice-cream) or meaningful (e.g., supporting a charity), preferably both, for us to invest our time and resources. The same applies to meditation. Meditation on the breath or a neutral word may be relaxing but can get boring after some time. Adding emotion to the practice makes it engaging and enjoyable. Earlier, we practiced the morning gratitude exercise, which adds the feeling of gratitude to meditation. An equally powerful practice is meditating on kindness.

Kindness (or compassion) meditation is one of the most powerful forms of meditation. It is relatively easy to learn. Further, as little as seven minutes of practice shows a positive effect on relationships with others.

Try starting your kindness meditation practice where it is likely to be effortless: with someone you love who you know is struggling. Gradually you can extend your kindness toward those you don't know very well, toward yourself, and even those who might be annoying.

The hope is that practicing kindness in the quiet of your mind will start changing how you interact with others and the self.

An important suggestion: Please be kind to yourself as you start your meditation practice. Just as you can't swim like a dolphin in a few weeks, meditation takes years of practice for it to become natural to you. Initially, you might spend the bulk of the time on the mat experiencing mind wandering. Hopefully, adding kindness to the practice will help your focus.

Further, it's helpful to remember that **the purpose of meditation is to be meditative when you aren't meditating.** The same applies to kind meditation. The goal isn't to see the light or achieve some exalted state. The goal is to become calmer and broaden your sphere of kindness.

All the different benefits of meditation—improved attention, emotional regulation, improved mood, better physical health, better relationships—apply to kindness meditation.[115]

Happy meditating!

Please watch the following videos if you are using this journal concurrent with the online program at resilientliving.net.

Module III: Kindness

Video #	Video Title
30	Kind Meditation
31	The Two Brains
32	Module III Summary

Date: _____ / _____ / _____ *Day* _____

Today's Insight:
Kindness is one of the most efficient and effective feelings when it comes to accessing positivity. Just seven minutes of loving-kindness meditation can enhance social connection and positivity toward others, including strangers.[116]

Redefining strangers as potential future friends is an excellent way to look at the world. When meeting a phlebotomist, social worker, or someone in the elevator, try to seem them within their circle of love. Try to see them as someone's spouse, parent, child, sibling, friend, nephew, or niece, and not just as a professional.

When you see others at a deeper level, you start valuing them more. The good energy is reflected in your facial expressions, demeanor, and words. They respond in kind, creating a nice feedback loop that helps you spread kindness in your and others' world.

Practices	Set Intention	Assess Action
Morning Gratitude	☐	☐
Grateful Memories	☐	☐
Curious Moments	☐	☐
The Two-Minute Rule	☐	☐
Kind Attention	☐	☐
Kind Meditation I'll send silent, kind thoughts in my meditation to at least four people.	☐	☐

Reflection:
My reflections for today:_____

_____

Think of what made you happy before you learned to get sad.
It will give you an idea of how to be happy again.

 *Date: _____ / _____ / _____ Day _____*

Today's Insight:
When someone doesn't smile at me, I assume they are upset or don't like me anymore. When someone doesn't respond to my text, I believe they don't think I am important. When no one talks to me at a party, I feel purposefully neglected. Despite years of working on myself, my instinct is to assume negative intent. I am susceptible to biases and prejudices.

Research shows kindness meditation effectively decreases prejudices.[117] Removal of prejudices frees up your brain so you can focus on connecting with others at a deeper level. They feel your deeper presence and feel validated in your presence.

The kinder you are, the more people wish to connect with you. Your kindness expands your circle of connection and love. Embodying kindness through challenging times inspires others to embrace kindness, starting a wave that may travel much farther than you can know or imagine.

Practices	Set Intention	Assess Action
Morning Gratitude	☐	☐
Grateful Memories	☐	☐
Curious Moments	☐	☐
The Two-Minute Rule	☐	☐
Kind Attention	☐	☐
Kind Meditation I'll send silent, kind thoughts in my meditation to at least four people.	☐	☐

Reflection:
My reflections for today:_____

_____

_____

Others value you not as you are but as they are. Giving them the power to influence your self-worth is giving away too much control.

Date: _____ / _____ / _____ Day _____

Today's Insight:
Disruptions are stressful. During the difficult times, we struggle to maintain composure, patience, and peace. These are, however, the most powerful times because these are also the moments that provide us an opportunity for growth. Disruptions that do not diminish love take us to greater heights.

None of this would happen on its own. Every transformation needs intentional effort. Kindness meditation also requires some effort initially. But the effort plateaus with time.[118]

One suggestion is to free up the time from unnecessary busy-ness. Examine your day and see if you are spending too much time watching the news or engaged om another activity that doesn't add value. Time is a zero-sum game. Our most precious asset is the number of heartbeats we have. Swap a less meaningful activity with something truly meaningful .

Practices	Set Intention	Assess Action
Morning Gratitude	☐	☐
Grateful Memories	☐	☐
Curious Moments	☐	☐
The Two-Minute Rule	☐	☐
Kind Attention	☐	☐
Kind Meditation I'll send silent, kind thoughts in my meditation to at least four people.	☐	☐

Reflection:
My reflections for today:_____

_____

_____

> *Increasing good thoughts is easier than eliminating the bad ones.*
> *Crowd your mind and life with the good. The bad will slowly fade.*

Date: _____ / _____ / _____ *Day* _____

Today's Insight:
Scientists estimate that only a small part of the energy in the universe (~5 percent) is presently visible. The rest is all invisible to scientific instruments. The same applies to suffering. We experience a lot of suffering in the quiet of our mind.[119,120] The regrets, rejections, and hurts of the past, the concerns and fears of the future—these feelings occupy a large silent part of our day.

Live one day assuming everyone in front of you is lifting an emotional weight heavier than he or she can carry. For this day, let go of any comparisons. Many people who have everything going well in their lives and have no reason to be unhappy, feel miserable. With this realization, keep a low threshold to forgive.

The day we realize the universality of human struggles will be the day we will develop universal compassion, and with that lasting peace.

Practices	Set Intention	Assess Action
Morning Gratitude	☐	☐
Grateful Memories	☐	☐
Curious Moments	☐	☐
The Two-Minute Rule	☐	☐
Kind Attention	☐	☐
Kind Meditation I'll send silent, kind thoughts in my meditation to at least four people.	☐	☐

Reflection:
My reflections for today:_____
_____

_____

Forgiving someone at work improves your relationships at home.
Forgiving someone at home improves your performance at work.

Date: _____ / _____ / _____ *Day* _____

Today's Insight:
All of us have multiple roles we fulfill—loved one, parent, child, friend, colleague, client, neighbor, and more. While at this moment, we may be serving a defined purpose, perhaps in the past, we had a very different identity. A war hero or a graduate of an Ivy League college isn't guaranteed lasting success. Life circumstances entirely beyond one's control can place anyone in a downward spiral.

Individual accountability is essential, but it's good to know that a person who is finding it tough to get by may be struggling through no fault of his or her own. Such a perspective will bring you the deepest compassion.[121]

A kinder perspective doesn't mean that you have to go around hugging every homeless person. But perhaps it is healthy to remember that many of them are war veterans to whom we are grateful for our freedom.

Practices	Set Intention	Assess Action
Morning Gratitude	☐	☐
Grateful Memories	☐	☐
Curious Moments	☐	☐
The Two-Minute Rule	☐	☐
Kind Attention	☐	☐
Kind Meditation I'll send silent, kind thoughts in my meditation to at least four people.	☐	☐

Reflection:
My reflections for today:_____

_____

Our effort and intentions not the outcomes are in our control.
Peg your self-worth on effort and intentions, and not the outcomes.

Date: _____ / _____ / _____ *Day* _____

Today's Insight:
Two constant companions of many adversities are chronic pain and lack of restorative sleep. Research shows that it takes superhuman effort to remain kind when you haven't slept well and are in pain.[122] Lack of kindness worsens your relationship with others, leading to further stressful situations.

Best to understand and accept this vulnerability, and not judge yourself, if while feeling unwell, you struggle giving out compassion. Next, remind yourself that while your annoyance is justified, it isn't helpful. A good skill I find useful is to see someone annoying as very young or very old. When you recall that the annoying person in front you must have been a newborn at some point and will be a vulnerable elderly person in the future, and look at the other person in that light, it will be easier to find kindness in your heart. That may be the start of a more nurturing relationship with the other person and the self.

Practices	Set Intention	Assess Action
Morning Gratitude	☐	☐
Grateful Memories	☐	☐
Curious Moments	☐	☐
The Two-Minute Rule	☐	☐
Kind Attention	☐	☐
Kind Meditation I'll send silent, kind thoughts in my meditation to at least four people.	☐	☐

Reflection:
My reflections for today:_____

_____

_____

If we all think, speak, and behave the way we want our children to think, speak, and behave, the world will be a much better place.

71

Today's Insight:
Our mind is like a mirror. It reflects what we shine on it. The most recent experience tends to dominate the mind. Further, when you crowd the mind with the positive, the negative may not find any space.

When you prime your mind with hopeful stories, the mind becomes more hopeful; priming the mind with negative stories worsens the mood.[123] If you can, choose to read uplifting stories that remind you of the highest places the human spirit can go.

Keep a low threshold for celebrating. Celebrate the milestones instead of waiting to party at the project's completion. Enjoy the 60 percent clearance sale, the chance encounter with an old friend, the completion of one wall of the dollhouse, and more.[124]

In addition, keep someone inspiring in your thoughts, someone who, despite struggles, embraced life, and chose to live by impeccable values.

Practices	Set Intention	Assess Action
Morning Gratitude	☐	☐
Grateful Memories	☐	☐
Curious Moments	☐	☐
The Two-Minute Rule	☐	☐
Kind Attention	☐	☐
Kind Meditation I'll send silent, kind thoughts in my meditation to at least four people.	☐	☐

Reflection:
My reflections for today:_____

_____

Believe in, and remind yourself of this powerful mantra each day:
"I am enough. I have enough."

Week 7: Resilient Mindset

On the right, you see a brain looking at a donut. Three different areas of the brain are evaluating the donut:

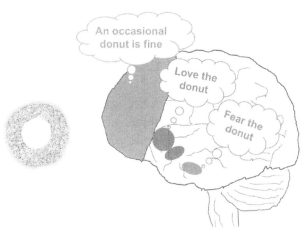

- The reward network loves the donut
- The fear network is afraid of the donut
- The prefrontal cortex thinks an occasional donut is fine

Do you see how **different areas of the brain conflict with each other**? They all give input based on the task entrusted to them. No other part of the body is conflicted like this. Hence the need for a construct that we can trust.

After much researching and thinking, I have found five principles that are timeless and validated by science. **Together these principles are like a GPS for the mind. They are gratitude, compassion, acceptance, meaning, and forgiveness.** One way we integrate these principles into our lives is by assigning each of them a day of the week as below:

Monday	Gratitude
Tuesday	Compassion
Wednesday	Acceptance
Thursday	Meaning
Friday	Forgiveness

To complete the week, Saturdays are the days of celebration, and Sundays are the days of reflection/prayer.

The purpose of assigning a day to each principle isn't to become nerdy about it. You don't say, "I can't be compassionate on Thursdays, since Tuesday is my day of compassion!" The purpose is to give an initial anchor to your thoughts as you integrate these principles into your life.

For example, on a Tuesday, spend more time reading, thinking, writing, and speaking about compassion. As your skills develop, you will be able to pick any of the principles that make the most sense to you at a given time.

Gratitude

We all have the gratitude software within us. The key is to **move from waiting to be grateful for something big to choosing gratitude for something small.**

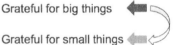

Ungrateful

Grateful for big things

Grateful for small things

Simply grateful

Grateful for adversity

Once, as I was eating a pear, I looked at the stalk of the pear and thought of its importance in making the pear happen. If I am grateful for the pear, why not be thankful also for the stalk.

Even deeper than being grateful for the small things is to be simply grateful without needing anything external. In this image, both are grateful to each other—like most life exchanges. It is similar to the relationship between a bee and the flower.

The deepest level of gratitude is to be grateful even for adversity. The classic example is that of Matthew Henry, a Bible scholar in 17th century England. After being robbed in the

streets of London, he felt grateful that it was the first time he was robbed and that he was the one robbed, not the one doing the robbing. He was also grateful that he wasn't physically hurt in the act.

A word of caution: **Avoid fast-tracking to gratitude in adversity. Gratitude amidst deep sorrow may feel phony.** In such situations, it is better to focus on connection, validation, self-compassion, and, if you wish, prayer.

Compassion

In thinking about compassion, it is important to distinguish between empathy and compassion.

Empathy is understanding and feeling another person's pain. Compassion, in addition, is validating the other person,

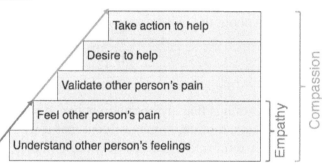

nurturing a desire to help, and taking action to support. **Empathy is an internal feeling, while compassion is external action. Empathy can worsen your mood, while compassion is uplifting.** Two simple ways to enhance compassion are API and finding commonalities.

API: When dealing with disagreements, at work, or in our personal lives, we often assume that we are entirely right and the other person doesn't "get it." My previous default was Assume Negative Intent (ANI). I have tried to change it to Assume Positive Intent (API)—maybe the other

person knows something or has experienced something that I haven't. Maybe he or she is annoyed today because her child is unwell, he couldn't sleep well last night, she has a backache, or his blood test came back abnormal. Filling the moment with validating stories and good adjectives makes it easier to access this thought: **"An expression other than love is a call for help."**

Finding commonalities: **The more commonalities you can find with the other person, the greater your compassion for them.** If you didn't try this earlier in the program, I suggest you try this practice now. Check all the boxes that apply to you:

Been to Canada	☐	Love chocolate	☐
Behind on sleep	☐	Want to plant more trees	☐
Concerned about the children	☐	Not disciplined about flossing	☐
Love pets	☐	Prefer paper over plastic	☐

These are the things that are common between you and me that we figured out in less than a minute. I am confident that if we sat together for twenty minutes, we would find hundreds of commonalities. The more commonalities we find, the greater our compassion for each other. Think about this for someone who annoys you!

Self-compassion: **Self-compassion is treating yourself with kindness and grace.** It is a combination of feeling worthy of receiving kindness and being kind to the self. We often aren't kind to ourselves because we worry that self-compassion will lower our standards. We sometimes carry lofty expectations of ourselves and also pay more attention to those who don't value us. Here are four ideas to enhance self-compassion:

- Believe in those who believe in you.
- Focus more on effort and intentions, and not the outcome.

- Anchor your self-worth in the principles you embody and not other things that are more transient.
- Spend more time with people who are truly happy in your happiness and accept you as you are.

Pick at least one of the ideas that makes sense to you and consider implementing it in your thought process.

Acceptance

Acceptance is often confused with apathy, which is passive giving up. Acceptance is the opposite. **It is an empowered engagement.** Consider this example. You are sitting at home watching your favorite TV show. The doorbell rings, and a teenager is selling cookies to raise money for an animal shelter. You aren't much into cookies. What will you do? Buy a box  or two or shove the door in her face? The answer is obvious.

The skill you used was acceptance, which is creatively working with what is. Acceptance chooses the right battles, ones that are worthy of your time. Acceptance also recognizes that a lot in life is beyond our control. Instead of lamenting about the untimely rain (or snow in Minnesota), it might be best to save the energy to open the umbrella.

The two aspects of acceptance are with people and situations.

Accepting people: The chances are that you have someone in your life whose peculiarities get on your nerves. **An excellent way to inspire others to change is to accept them as they are.** Three ways to accept others are:
- Focusing on gratitude for what is right about them
- Finding a rational context in what seems wrong

- Finding meaning in what seems wrong

Accepting situations: When you put seeds in three planters, one of them grows flowers, the other grows nothing, while the third one produces weeds. It's always helpful to investigate how to grow more flowers yet recognize that not all weeds can be

eliminated. If the growing season is behind us, then it is best to celebrate the flowers instead of mourning the weeds.

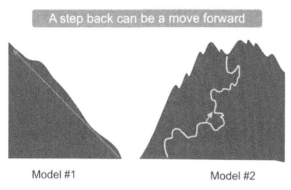

A step back can be a move forward

Model #1   Model #2

Another simple metaphor in acceptance is to recognize that **the climb on a mountain is seldom straight up** (Model #1). You may take two steps forward and then one step backward (Model #2). This awareness will help you keep your hopes alive when the progress feels small or immeasurable.

Meaning

The ultimate meaning of life is difficult to ascertain. Life, to me, feels like reading an infinite novel. No one I know has read the last page. Maybe there isn't any last page. The moment we close a chapter, another one starts, even though we can't see it right now. When walking into the

fog, you can't see ten miles ahead. But you can see the next hundred feet. So, asking what the ultimate meaning of life is may not be the best question. **A better question is—"How can I make my life more meaningful?"**

Meaning plays out in two ways.

Reactive: Reactive meaning is a way of reframing adversity. For example, if you have a flat tire, can you notice that there is no other damage, the car is in a parking lot, it's day time, and you are likely in a safe neighborhood? **This is a way of focusing on what could have gone wrong but didn't.**

Proactive: Your North star is a purpose that you care about the most. Around this purpose, you can organize all your efforts. Proactive meaning helps you live with that purpose.

For example, my personal North star is children. **It doesn't matter who gives me my paycheck. My employer is all the children of the world.** I hope to help build a better world for them.

Your proactive meaning plays out in three domains: Relationships, Work, and Spirituality. Successful integration of these three meanings can be

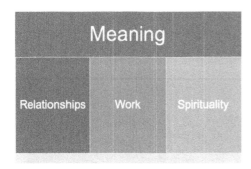

Meaning

Relationships | Work | Spirituality

your recipe for a fulfilling life. Access additional writings if you wish to go deeper into meaning.

Forgiveness
Perhaps the most essential part of forgiveness is to understand that **it is for you more than the forgiven. By forgiving, you give others an eviction notice from your brain's rental space.**

The joy of revenge: **Forgiveness is difficult because our brain believes that the instinct of revenge will keep us safe.** Why is that? As the image below shows, we weren't kind to each other in our ancestral past.

What forgiveness isn't

- Justifying
- Condoning
- Excusing
- Denying

What forgiveness is

- A voluntary choice
- For you
- Practicing your principles
- Often goes to the undeserving

Forgiveness was a sign of the weak. That's why contemplating revenge activates our brain's pleasure center.

Two ideas: Forgiveness isn't easy, and for the more egregious hurts, you might need

help from your loved ones, friends, and professionals. Two simple starter ideas for the lighter hurts are:

#1. Remove intentionality: When I stepped on my dog (her name was Moni), she turned around and bit my hand. How can I blame Moni? She acted out of self-defense. Maybe the person who hurt you didn't know better or acted out of fear. **The more you can remove intentionality, the easier it will be to forgive.**

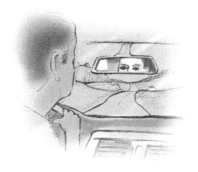

#2. Rise in your eyes: When you look at your reflection, who do you see? If you want to see the eyes of your role model, then consider forgiveness because most inspiring people in the world choose to forgive, at least the minor insults.

Resilient mindset invites you to integrate the above five principles using one or more of the following approaches:

- ◊ **Read** about the principle—through one of the books from many wonderful authors, online programs, and web searches.
- ◊ **Think** about the principle—Think about what gratitude or compassion means to you, how forgiveness can enhance your life, how meaning connects with your version of spirituality, and how you can integrate these principles into your daily routine.
- ◊ **Write** about the principle—Write in your journal, on paper, or online.
- ◊ **Share** the principle—Buddy up with someone and mutually support your progress as you start a lifelong journey of learning and healing.
- ◊ **Practice** the principle—The above text provides a few starter ideas. I have shared many more ideas in the accompanying online program (resilientliving.net) and the book (*SMART with Dr. Sood*).

Let's continue with week 7 of our journey together.

Please watch the following videos (you have many more to watch this week) if you are using this journal concurrent with the online program at resilientliving.net.

Module IV: Resilient Mindset

Video #	Video Title
33	Mindset: The Conflicted Design
34	The Five Principles
35	Gratitude: Lower the Threshold
36	Gratitude: Even Deeper
37	Compassion versus Empathy
38	Compassion Practice: Two Ideas
39	Self-Compassion
40	Acceptance: Buy those Cookies
41	Intentional Non-Acceptance
42	Accepting People: Three Insights
43	Accepting People: Three Ideas
44	Meaning: A Better Question
45	Meaning: Your North Star
46	Forgiveness: What is it?
47	Cultivating Forgiveness: Two Ideas
48	Pre-emptive Forgiveness
49	Summary of Part IV

Date: _____ / _____ / _____ *Day* _____

Today's Insight:
Cut a branch off a tree, and it will grow another. Block the light from one side, and the tree will tilt to the other. Trees instinctively know how to seek the light. I can't say the same about me on most days. I still haven't fully forgiven my rude tenth grade math teacher.

Let's think about what children with disabilities do at school. Their teachers tell me that the kids with some limitations are the happiest. They give their best effort and seldom complain. They focus on their abilities and not on their disabilities.

Let's feel inspired by these little sages who remind us that the greatest joy isn't in achieving but in striving. And if one corner of your life has gone dark, spend more time looking at the corner that is still well lit.

Practices	Set Intention	Assess Action
Morning Gratitude	☐	☐
Grateful Memories	☐	☐
Curious Moments	☐	☐
The Two-Minute Rule	☐	☐
Kind Attention	☐	☐
Kind Meditation	☐	☐
Resilient Thinking I'll align my thoughts with one or more of these five principles: Gratitude, Compassion, Acceptance, Meaning, Forgiveness	☐	☐

Reflection:
My reflections for today:_____

_____

Revisit kind & happy memories by rethinking them often. Think more about people who lift your self-worth, not the ones who judge you.

Date: _____ / _____ / _____ *Day* _____

Today's Insight:
A very successful singer developed several medical problems. As a result, he lost his voice. After intensive medical treatment, his voice improved, but he wasn't anywhere close to his best self. He had also lost his confidence and felt judged by people close to him.

"Who loves you unconditionally and accepts you just as you are?" I asked.

"My grandma," he said.

"Then sing for your grandma."

"But she has passed away."

"Then imagine she is sitting in the audience admiring your singing."

He did just that and in a few months, found his voice.

Look at yourself with the eyes of someone who loves you unconditionally. That's a great way to awaken your best self.

Practices	Set Intention	Assess Action
Morning Gratitude	☐	☐
Grateful Memories	☐	☐
Curious Moments	☐	☐
The Two-Minute Rule	☐	☐
Kind Attention	☐	☐
Kind Meditation	☐	☐
Resilient Thinking I'll align my thoughts with one or more of these five principles: Gratitude, Compassion, Acceptance, Meaning, Forgiveness	☐	☐

Reflection:
My reflections for today:_____

_____

Believe in those who believe in you.
You are who your pet thinks you are.

Today's Insight:

A friend of mine, diagnosed with advanced cancer, has undergone extensive surgery and chemotherapy. Despite struggles with ongoing symptoms, he is fully engaged with life and keeps an upbeat spirit. He is back to work, which he finds therapeutic. He is inspiring others to achieve their highest potential despite the obstacles and setbacks.

"How do you find all the energy?" I asked.

"I don't fight the symptoms," he said. "I use my energy to fight the disease. I believe discomfort is necessary for healing."

He has taught me the true meaning of acceptance: to save your energy by choosing which fights are worth fighting and which ones are best avoided.

Practices	Set Intention	Assess Action
Morning Gratitude	☐	☐
Grateful Memories	☐	☐
Curious Moments	☐	☐
The Two-Minute Rule	☐	☐
Kind Attention	☐	☐
Kind Meditation	☐	☐
Resilient Thinking I'll align my thoughts with one or more of these five principles: Gratitude, Compassion, Acceptance, Meaning, Forgiveness	☐	☐

Reflection:

My reflections for today:_____

_____

A candle, when it burns, brings light to the room. The pain you are enduring today will bring light to people's lives.

Today's Insight:
Our planet is a tiny speck in an unimaginably vast universe. Scientists estimate that every single day, the universe spawns nearly 300 million new stars. Understanding our place in the universe fills me with humility.

While the ultimate meaning isn't easy to understand, a considerable part of our journey is experiencing happiness and love through sharing it.

We experience life at two levels—material and spiritual. Both are important and meaningful. It helps, however, to remember that we are a spiritual beings having a spiritual experience. It is in the integration of the material and the spiritual that we can realize our meaning.

Practices	Set Intention	Assess Action
Morning Gratitude	☐	☐
Grateful Memories	☐	☐
Curious Moments	☐	☐
The Two-Minute Rule	☐	☐
Kind Attention	☐	☐
Kind Meditation	☐	☐
Resilient Thinking I'll align my thoughts with one or more of these five principles: Gratitude, Compassion, Acceptance, Meaning, Forgiveness	☐	☐

Reflection:
My reflections for today:_____

_____

_____

A million likes on social media are no match for a few loving, trusting relationships.

Date: _____ / _____ / _____ *Day* _____

Today's Insight:
The full moon looks gorgeous to the unaided eye. But the moment we zoom in with binoculars, we start noticing the scars. The same applies to people. They might look perfect from a distance, but the more we know them, the more imperfections and annoyances we might discover.

Knowing this and adjusting your expectations, assuming others have constraints and aren't intentionally choosing to be selfish, annoying, or hurtful, will help with forgiveness.[125]

Faith makes forgiveness more accessible.[126] Praying for the self, others, for peace, healing, wisdom, and deeper faith—all enhance forgiveness.

Practices	Set Intention	Assess Action
Morning Gratitude	☐	☐
Grateful Memories	☐	☐
Curious Moments	☐	☐
The Two-Minute Rule	☐	☐
Kind Attention	☐	☐
Kind Meditation	☐	☐
Resilient Thinking I'll align my thoughts with one or more of these five principles: Gratitude, Compassion, Acceptance, Meaning, Forgiveness	☐	☐

Reflection:
My reflections for today:_____

_____

_____

> *Forgive in honor of those who were hurt*
> *worse than you, yet still chose to forgive.*

Date: _____ / _____ / _____ Day _____

Today's Insight:
While sharing others' difficult moments is an act of compassion, an equally important compassion practice is to share joy. Sometimes, joy is more difficult to share than sorrow, particularly with someone who may have been our competitor.

Celebrate the simple things in life—of yours and others'. Savor the morning sun, the dew drops on the grass, the birds visiting your feeder, the giggle of a young child, the half birthdays, the food on the plate, and more. These small moments decorate our days and are worth noticing, so life doesn't pass us by while we are busy clearing the weeds.

Ask for more details when others share something positive about their life. Your genuine interest and enthusiasm will double their joy and also yours.

Practices	Set Intention	Assess Action
Morning Gratitude	☐	☐
Grateful Memories	☐	☐
Curious Moments	☐	☐
The Two-Minute Rule	☐	☐
Kind Attention	☐	☐
Kind Meditation	☐	☐
Resilient Thinking I'll align my thoughts with one or more of these five principles: Gratitude, Compassion, Acceptance, Meaning, Forgiveness	☐	☐

Reflection:
My reflections for today:_____

_____

_____

Impatience slows progress & accelerates aging. Practice patience in daily life. Load the dishwasher as if it were a jewelry box!

Date: _____ / _____ / _____ *Day* _____

Today's Insight:
Consider using some time today to think deeper. Think about your life's journey, about the lives you have touched, and the ones that have touched you. Every exchange of ours is like that of a bee and a flower; it involves mutual sharing of service and love.

You serve when helping others; you also serve when you are being helped—by giving others meaning and by expressing authentic gratitude.

You love by giving undivided attention, through connection, compassion and caring, and through prayer. I once heard that meditation is listening to God, while prayer is talking to God. Listen and talk today from a deeper place with a grateful heart and a compassionate mind.

Practices	Set Intention	Assess Action
Morning Gratitude	☐	☐
Grateful Memories	☐	☐
Curious Moments	☐	☐
The Two-Minute Rule	☐	☐
Kind Attention	☐	☐
Kind Meditation	☐	☐
Resilient Thinking I'll align my thoughts with one or more of these five principles: Gratitude, Compassion, Acceptance, Meaning, Forgiveness	☐	☐

Reflection:
My reflections for today:_____
_____
_____

The best way to be happy is to be a source of happiness. The best way to be a source of happiness is to seek it for someone else.

Week 8: Your Preferred Practice

The seven practices covered so far constitute the core of our resilience approach. During this week, I invite you to implement your own preferred practice that we haven't covered or have only partially covered so far. Also, consider engaging with the following inspirational exercise.

Write the names of three people in your personal life you really admire.

1. _____

2. _____

3. _____

What are the top few qualities you admire in these people?

1. _____

2. _____

3. _____

Suggested activities for the next week:
- ◊ *Keep at least one person from the above list in your morning gratitude practice.*
- ◊ *Send a message of gratitude to all of these people at least once during the week. It could be a handwritten grateful note, an email, a text, or a small gift.*

Instructions for weeks 8-12: *For the coming weeks, the journal will not provide an insight for each day. Instead, the goal is for you to write your own insights based on how you are experiencing the world.*

I have provided additional space on the page for you to write your thoughts. You are welcome to read the SMART book or another text for starter ideas.

Also, once a day, consider writing a quote of your own. You could start from scratch or simply rephrase the quote you read at the bottom of the page in your own words.

Please watch the following video if you are using this journal concurrent with the online program at resilientliving.net. Consider watching the previous videos (videos 1-49) in this and subsequent weeks.

Final Thoughts

Video #	Video Title
50	Final Thoughts

 *Date*: _____ / _____ / _____ *Day* _____

Practices	Set Intention	Assess Action
Morning Gratitude	☐	☐
Grateful Memories	☐	☐
Curious Moments	☐	☐
The Two-Minute Rule	☐	☐
Kind Attention	☐	☐
Kind Meditation	☐	☐
Resilient Thinking	☐	☐
My Preferred Practice I'll implement the following practice:	☐	☐

Reflection:
My reflections for today:_____

_____

_____

_____

_____

_____

Quote:
My quote for today:_____

_____

_____

> *Resilience is a combination of strength and flexibility.*
> *Be flexible about the preferences and strong about the principles.*

Date: _____ / _____ / _____ *Day* _____

Practices	Set Intention	Assess Action
Morning Gratitude	☐	☐
Grateful Memories	☐	☐
Curious Moments	☐	☐
The Two-Minute Rule	☐	☐
Kind Attention	☐	☐
Kind Meditation	☐	☐
Resilient Thinking	☐	☐
My Preferred Practice I'll implement the following practice:	☐	☐

Reflection:
My reflections for today:_____

_____

_____

_____

_____

_____

Quote:
My quote for today:_____

_____

_____

> *You are an agent of service and love, helping build*
> *a kinder and happier world for our planet's children.*

Date: _____ / _____ / _____ *Day* _____

Practices	Set Intention	Assess Action
Morning Gratitude	☐	☐
Grateful Memories	☐	☐
Curious Moments	☐	☐
The Two-Minute Rule	☐	☐
Kind Attention	☐	☐
Kind Meditation	☐	☐
Resilient Thinking	☐	☐
My Preferred Practice I'll implement the following practice:	☐	☐

Reflection:
My reflections for today:_____

_____

_____

_____

_____

_____

Quote:
My quote for today:_____

_____

*If we must shovel the snow, it helps to remember that
snow is the water that we will get to drink in the summer.*

Date: _____ / _____ / _____ *Day* _____

Practices	Set Intention	Assess Action
Morning Gratitude	☐	☐
Grateful Memories	☐	☐
Curious Moments	☐	☐
The Two-Minute Rule	☐	☐
Kind Attention	☐	☐
Kind Meditation	☐	☐
Resilient Thinking	☐	☐
My Preferred Practice I'll implement the following practice:	☐	☐

Reflection:
My reflections for today:_____

_____

_____

_____

_____

Quote:
My quote for today:_____

_____

_____

Sometimes a hurt hurled at us is the other
person's misguided efforts toward self-protection.

Date: _____ / _____ / _____ Day _____

Practices	Set Intention	Assess Action
Morning Gratitude	☐	☐
Grateful Memories	☐	☐
Curious Moments	☐	☐
The Two-Minute Rule	☐	☐
Kind Attention	☐	☐
Kind Meditation	☐	☐
Resilient Thinking	☐	☐
My Preferred Practice I'll implement the following practice:	☐	☐

Reflection:
My reflections for today:_____

_____

_____

_____

_____

Quote:
My quote for today:_____

_____

_____

> *Fear blocks self-destructive courage, while courage checks*
> *paralyzing fear. We need both fear and courage, in balance.*

 *Date:* _____ / _____ / _____ *Day* _____

Practices	Set Intention	Assess Action
Morning Gratitude	☐	☐
Grateful Memories	☐	☐
Curious Moments	☐	☐
The Two-Minute Rule	☐	☐
Kind Attention	☐	☐
Kind Meditation	☐	☐
Resilient Thinking	☐	☐
My Preferred Practice I'll implement the following practice:	☐	☐

Reflection:
My reflections for today:_____

_____

_____

_____

_____

_____

Quote:
My quote for today:_____

_____

_____

> *Find novelty within the familiar to keep life interesting,*
> *and familiarity within the novel so you don't get overwhelmed.*

Date: _____ / _____ / _____ *Day* _____

Practices	Set Intention	Assess Action
Morning Gratitude	☐	☐
Grateful Memories	☐	☐
Curious Moments	☐	☐
The Two-Minute Rule	☐	☐
Kind Attention	☐	☐
Kind Meditation	☐	☐
Resilient Thinking	☐	☐
My Preferred Practice I'll implement the following practice:	☐	☐

Reflection:
My reflections for today:_____

_____

_____

_____

_____

_____

Quote:
My quote for today:_____

_____

_____

> *The light you bring into the lives of others*
> *simultaneously illuminates your own life.*

Week 9: Your Relationships

Write the names of three people in your personal life you feel are currently struggling (from medical, personal, professional, or other issues).

1. _____

2. _____

3. _____

What are a few similarities between you and these people?

1. _____

2. _____

3. _____

Suggested activities for the next week:

◊ *Keep at least one person from the above list in your morning gratitude practice. Assume that by sending this person your silent gratitude, you have protected this person for the week.*

◊ *Practice kind meditation each day and include at least one person from the above list in your meditation practice.*

◊ *Research the benefits of the following:*

   ○ *Having a strong sense of purpose*
   ○ *Positive social connections*
   ○ *Helping others (Volunteering)*
   ○ *Forgiveness*

Consider re-visiting some of the previous videos (videos 1-50) at resilientliving.net. We will do our best to post additional videos that are aligned with the theme and the spirit of the program you have experienced so far.

Date: _____ / _____ / _____ *Day* _____

Practices	Set Intention	Assess Action
Morning Gratitude	☐	☐
Grateful Memories	☐	☐
Curious Moments	☐	☐
The Two-Minute Rule	☐	☐
Kind Attention	☐	☐
Kind Meditation	☐	☐
Resilient Thinking	☐	☐
	☐	☐

Reflection:
My reflections for today:_____

_____

_____

_____

_____

Quote:
My quote for today:_____

_____

_____

> *On the road and in life, best not to drive
> looking into the rear-view mirror all the time.*

Date: _____ / _____ / _____ *Day* _____

Practices	Set Intention	Assess Action
Morning Gratitude	☐	☐
Grateful Memories	☐	☐
Curious Moments	☐	☐
The Two-Minute Rule	☐	☐
Kind Attention	☐	☐
Kind Meditation	☐	☐
Resilient Thinking	☐	☐
	☐	☐

Reflection:
My reflections for today:_____

_____

_____

_____

_____

_____

Quote:
My quote for today:_____

_____

*Forgiveness heals the past, lifts
the present, and brightens the future.*

Date: _____ / _____ / _____ Day _____

Practices	Set Intention	Assess Action
Morning Gratitude	☐	☐
Grateful Memories	☐	☐
Curious Moments	☐	☐
The Two-Minute Rule	☐	☐
Kind Attention	☐	☐
Kind Meditation	☐	☐
Resilient Thinking	☐	☐
	☐	☐

Reflection:
My reflections for today:_____

_____

_____

_____

_____

_____

Quote:
My quote for today:_____

_____

Acting superior is a reflection of feeling inferior. The hallmark of a phenomenal person is his or her phenomenal humility.

Date: _____ / _____ / _____ *Day* _____

Practices	Set Intention	Assess Action
Morning Gratitude	☐	☐
Grateful Memories	☐	☐
Curious Moments	☐	☐
The Two-Minute Rule	☐	☐
Kind Attention	☐	☐
Kind Meditation	☐	☐
Resilient Thinking	☐	☐
	☐	☐

Reflection:

My reflections for today:_____

_____

_____

_____

_____

_____

Quote:

My quote for today:_____

_____

> *Most people handle future adversity much better than they imagined. So it is best to use the energy to prepare and not fear.*

Date: _____ / _____ / _____ *Day* _____

Practices	Set Intention	Assess Action
Morning Gratitude	☐	☐
Grateful Memories	☐	☐
Curious Moments	☐	☐
The Two-Minute Rule	☐	☐
Kind Attention	☐	☐
Kind Meditation	☐	☐
Resilient Thinking	☐	☐
	☐	☐

Reflection:
My reflections for today:_____

_____

_____

_____

_____

_____

Quote:
My quote for today:_____

_____

Forgive yourself if you don't have a PhD in human relationships and life's struggles. None of us do.

Date: _____ / _____ / _____ *Day* _____

Practices	Set Intention	Assess Action
Morning Gratitude	☐	☐
Grateful Memories	☐	☐
Curious Moments	☐	☐
The Two-Minute Rule	☐	☐
Kind Attention	☐	☐
Kind Meditation	☐	☐
Resilient Thinking	☐	☐
	☐	☐

Reflection:
My reflections for today:_____

_____

_____

_____

_____

_____

Quote:
My quote for today:_____

_____

_____

Happiness = Reality – Expectations

Date: _____ / _____ / _____ *Day* _____

Practices	Set Intention	Assess Action
Morning Gratitude	☐	☐
Grateful Memories	☐	☐
Curious Moments	☐	☐
The Two-Minute Rule	☐	☐
Kind Attention	☐	☐
Kind Meditation	☐	☐
Resilient Thinking	☐	☐
	☐	☐

Reflection:
My reflections for today:_____

_____

_____

_____

_____

_____

Quote:
My quote for today:_____

_____

Assume everyone is phenomenally interesting
and precious. See them in their circle of love.

Week 10: Hope

Read the chapter on hope at resilientliving.net and then answer these three questions:

How do you define hope? _____

_____

_____

What are some of the benefits of being more hopeful?

_____

_____

_____

_____

How can you become more hopeful?

_____

_____

_____

_____

_____

_____

_____

Consider re-visiting some of the previous videos (videos 1-50) at resilientliving.net. We will do our best to post additional videos that are aligned with the theme and the spirit of the program you have experienced so far.

Date: _____ / _____ / _____ *Day* _____

Practices	Set Intention	Assess Action
Morning Gratitude	☐	☐
Grateful Memories	☐	☐
Curious Moments	☐	☐
The Two-Minute Rule	☐	☐
Kind Attention	☐	☐
Kind Meditation	☐	☐
Resilient Thinking	☐	☐
	☐	☐

Reflection:
My reflections for today:_____

_____

_____

_____

_____

_____

Quote:
My quote for today:_____

_____

Research shows that the opposite of being patient isn't being impatient. It is getting anxious, angry, injured, sick, and miserable.

Date: _____ / _____ / _____ *Day* _____

Practices	Set Intention	Assess Action
Morning Gratitude	☐	☐
Grateful Memories	☐	☐
Curious Moments	☐	☐
The Two-Minute Rule	☐	☐
Kind Attention	☐	☐
Kind Meditation	☐	☐
Resilient Thinking	☐	☐
	☐	☐

Reflection:
My reflections for today:_____

_____

_____

_____

_____

_____

Quote:
My quote for today:_____

_____

_____

Do not discount the compliments that come your way.
We tend to trust the criticism but disown the compliments.

Date: _____ / _____ / _____ *Day* _____

Practices	Set Intention	Assess Action
Morning Gratitude	☐	☐
Grateful Memories	☐	☐
Curious Moments	☐	☐
The Two-Minute Rule	☐	☐
Kind Attention	☐	☐
Kind Meditation	☐	☐
Resilient Thinking	☐	☐
	☐	☐

Reflection:
My reflections for today:_____

_____

_____

_____

_____

_____

Quote:
My quote for today:_____

_____

_____

Resist the urge to immediately provide insight to someone who is hurting. Instead, provide validation, connection, support, and love.

 *Date*: _____ / _____ / _____ *Day* _____

Practices	Set Intention	Assess Action
Morning Gratitude	☐	☐
Grateful Memories	☐	☐
Curious Moments	☐	☐
The Two-Minute Rule	☐	☐
Kind Attention	☐	☐
Kind Meditation	☐	☐
Resilient Thinking	☐	☐
	☐	☐

Reflection:
My reflections for today:_____
_____
_____
_____
_____
_____

Quote:
My quote for today:_____
_____

Carefully choose which battles you wish to fight. Let go of the battles where the effort is greater than the reward from victory.

Date: _____ / _____ / _____ *Day* _____

Practices	Set Intention	Assess Action
Morning Gratitude	☐	☐
Grateful Memories	☐	☐
Curious Moments	☐	☐
The Two-Minute Rule	☐	☐
Kind Attention	☐	☐
Kind Meditation	☐	☐
Resilient Thinking	☐	☐
	☐	☐

Reflection:
My reflections for today:_____

_____

_____

_____

_____

_____

Quote:
My quote for today:_____

_____

*Feeling superior or feeling inferior both make
us vulnerable. The greatest joy is in feeling equal.*

Date: _____ / _____ / _____ *Day* _____

Practices	Set Intention	Assess Action
Morning Gratitude	☐	☐
Grateful Memories	☐	☐
Curious Moments	☐	☐
The Two-Minute Rule	☐	☐
Kind Attention	☐	☐
Kind Meditation	☐	☐
Resilient Thinking	☐	☐
	☐	☐

Reflection:
My reflections for today:_____

_____

_____

_____

_____

_____

Quote:
My quote for today:_____

_____

_____

In our pursuit of happiness, material wealth is a much less efficient solution than boosting compassion for others and ourselves.

Date: _____ / _____ / _____ *Day* _____

Practices	Set Intention	Assess Action
Morning Gratitude	☐	☐
Grateful Memories	☐	☐
Curious Moments	☐	☐
The Two-Minute Rule	☐	☐
Kind Attention	☐	☐
Kind Meditation	☐	☐
Resilient Thinking	☐	☐
	☐	☐

Reflection:
My reflections for today:_____

_____

_____

_____

_____

_____

Quote:
My quote for today:_____

_____

_____

Patients being cared by more compassionate physicians have shorter duration of illness and better immune response.

Week 11: Courage

Read the chapter on courage at resilientliving.net and then answer these three questions:

How do you define courage? _____

_____

_____

What are some of the benefits of being more courageous?

_____

_____

_____

_____

How can you become more courageous?

_____

_____

_____

_____

_____

_____

_____

Consider watching the previous videos (videos 1-50) at resilientliving.net. We will do our best to post additional videos that are aligned with the theme and the spirit of the program you have experienced so far.

Date: _____ / _____ / _____ *Day* _____

Practices	Set Intention	Assess Action
Morning Gratitude	☐	☐
Grateful Memories	☐	☐
Curious Moments	☐	☐
The Two-Minute Rule	☐	☐
Kind Attention	☐	☐
Kind Meditation	☐	☐
Resilient Thinking	☐	☐
	☐	☐

Reflection:
My reflections for today:_____

_____

_____

_____

_____

_____

Quote:
My quote for today:_____

_____

*Courage is recognizing that the meaning that drives
you is more powerful than the fears that hold you.*

Date: _____ / _____ / _____ *Day* _____

Practices	Set Intention	Assess Action
Morning Gratitude	☐	☐
Grateful Memories	☐	☐
Curious Moments	☐	☐
The Two-Minute Rule	☐	☐
Kind Attention	☐	☐
Kind Meditation	☐	☐
Resilient Thinking	☐	☐
	☐	☐

Reflection:
My reflections for today:_____

_____

_____

_____

_____

_____

Quote:
My quote for today:_____

_____

It takes greater courage to forgive than to take revenge.
Such courage ensures you end your life with fewer regrets.

Date: _____ / _____ / _____ Day _____

Practices	Set Intention	Assess Action
Morning Gratitude	☐	☐
Grateful Memories	☐	☐
Curious Moments	☐	☐
The Two-Minute Rule	☐	☐
Kind Attention	☐	☐
Kind Meditation	☐	☐
Resilient Thinking	☐	☐
	☐	☐

Reflection:
My reflections for today:_____

_____

_____

_____

_____

_____

Quote:
My quote for today:_____

_____

The courageous are good at managing fear. Courage is related more to the strength of your purpose than the power of your biceps.

Date: _____ / _____ / _____ *Day* _____

Practices	Set Intention	Assess Action
Morning Gratitude	☐	☐
Grateful Memories	☐	☐
Curious Moments	☐	☐
The Two-Minute Rule	☐	☐
Kind Attention	☐	☐
Kind Meditation	☐	☐
Resilient Thinking	☐	☐
	☐	☐

Reflection:
My reflections for today:_____

_____

_____

_____

_____

_____

Quote:
My quote for today:_____

_____

Fifty percent of your impatience is encoded in your genes. Blame your genes for your impatience, pat yourself on the back for your patience!

Date: _____ / _____ / _____ *Day* _____

Practices	Set Intention	Assess Action
Morning Gratitude	☐	☐
Grateful Memories	☐	☐
Curious Moments	☐	☐
The Two-Minute Rule	☐	☐
Kind Attention	☐	☐
Kind Meditation	☐	☐
Resilient Thinking	☐	☐
	☐	☐

Reflection:
My reflections for today:_____

_____

_____

_____

_____

_____

Quote:
My quote for today:_____

_____

> *Courage keeps the company of humility. For their heroic deeds, the courageous often say, "I was just doing my job."*

Date: _____ / _____ / _____ Day _____

Practices	Set Intention	Assess Action
Morning Gratitude	☐	☐
Grateful Memories	☐	☐
Curious Moments	☐	☐
The Two-Minute Rule	☐	☐
Kind Attention	☐	☐
Kind Meditation	☐	☐
Resilient Thinking	☐	☐
	☐	☐

Reflection:
My reflections for today:_____

_____

_____

_____

_____

_____

Quote:
My quote for today:_____

_____

_____

On a material level and for the short term, the world isn't fair. Bad things happen to good people and good things happen to bad people.

Date: _____ / _____ / _____ *Day* _____

Practices	Set Intention	Assess Action
Morning Gratitude	☐	☐
Grateful Memories	☐	☐
Curious Moments	☐	☐
The Two-Minute Rule	☐	☐
Kind Attention	☐	☐
Kind Meditation	☐	☐
Resilient Thinking	☐	☐
	☐	☐

Reflection:
My reflections for today:_____

_____

_____

_____

_____

Quote:
My quote for today:_____

_____

Forgiving can be very difficult. Forgetting is near impossible.
Be kind to yourself on your journey to forgiveness.

Week 12: Keep Growing

Write a few personal thoughts about what adversity has taught you that you wish to share with others, particularly in the light of our journey together over the past 11 weeks. Think about how you can continue to grow in the coming weeks and months.

_____

_____

_____

_____

_____

_____

_____

_____

_____

_____

_____

_____

_____

_____

Consider sharing your thoughts with me at as@resilientoption.com. I will strive my very best to respond to you. I wish you a life full of hope, healing, meaning, and nurturing connections.

Consider watching the previous videos (videos 1-50) at resilientliving.net. We will do our best to post additional videos that are aligned with the theme and the spirit of the program you have experienced so far.

Date: _____ / _____ / _____ *Day* _____

Practices	Set Intention	Assess Action
Morning Gratitude	☐	☐
Grateful Memories	☐	☐
Curious Moments	☐	☐
The Two-Minute Rule	☐	☐
Kind Attention	☐	☐
Kind Meditation	☐	☐
Resilient Thinking	☐	☐
	☐	☐

Reflection:
My reflections for today:_____

_____

_____

_____

_____

_____

Quote:
My quote for today:_____

_____

_____

With two-thirds of the earth covered with clouds, they will rain on you someday. You can't stop the rain but you can use an umbrella.

Date: _____ / _____ / _____ *Day* _____

Practices	Set Intention	Assess Action
Morning Gratitude	☐	☐
Grateful Memories	☐	☐
Curious Moments	☐	☐
The Two-Minute Rule	☐	☐
Kind Attention	☐	☐
Kind Meditation	☐	☐
Resilient Thinking	☐	☐
	☐	☐

Reflection:
My reflections for today:_____

_____

_____

_____

_____

_____

Quote:
My quote for today:_____

_____

No need to be embarrassed by your irrational thoughts. They are a norm for everyone. Just don't act on them & reduce their dose.

Date: _____ / _____ / _____ *Day* _____

Practices	Set Intention	Assess Action
Morning Gratitude	☐	☐
Grateful Memories	☐	☐
Curious Moments	☐	☐
The Two-Minute Rule	☐	☐
Kind Attention	☐	☐
Kind Meditation	☐	☐
Resilient Thinking	☐	☐
	☐	☐

Reflection:
My reflections for today:_____

_____

_____

_____

_____

Quote:
My quote for today:_____

_____

Our sources of stress and joy are the same.
Wishing away all the stressors would be wishing away life.

Date: _____ / _____ / _____ *Day* _____

Practices	Set Intention	Assess Action
Morning Gratitude	☐	☐
Grateful Memories	☐	☐
Curious Moments	☐	☐
The Two-Minute Rule	☐	☐
Kind Attention	☐	☐
Kind Meditation	☐	☐
Resilient Thinking	☐	☐
	☐	☐

Reflection:
My reflections for today:_____

_____

_____

_____

_____

_____

Quote:
My quote for today:_____

_____

Do not multitask in relationships.
Partial presence could be worse than absence.

Date: _____ / _____ / _____ *Day* _____

Practices	Set Intention	Assess Action
Morning Gratitude	☐	☐
Grateful Memories	☐	☐
Curious Moments	☐	☐
The Two-Minute Rule	☐	☐
Kind Attention	☐	☐
Kind Meditation	☐	☐
Resilient Thinking	☐	☐
	☐	☐

Reflection:
My reflections for today:_____

_____

_____

_____

_____

_____

Quote:
My quote for today:_____

_____

_____

A negative event assigned a positive meaning feels less negative.
However, the deeper the hurt, the longer it takes to find meaning.

Date: _____ / _____ / _____ *Day* _____

Practices	Set Intention	Assess Action
Morning Gratitude	☐	☐
Grateful Memories	☐	☐
Curious Moments	☐	☐
The Two-Minute Rule	☐	☐
Kind Attention	☐	☐
Kind Meditation	☐	☐
Resilient Thinking	☐	☐
	☐	☐

Reflection:
My reflections for today:_____

_____

_____

_____

_____

_____

Quote:
My quote for today:_____

_____

Gratitude and compassion are so beneficial that if they were a pill, we would be taking them three times a day and would not mind the copay.

Date: _____ / _____ / _____ *Day* _____

Practices	Set Intention	Assess Action
Morning Gratitude	☐	☐
Grateful Memories	☐	☐
Curious Moments	☐	☐
The Two-Minute Rule	☐	☐
Kind Attention	☐	☐
Kind Meditation	☐	☐
Resilient Thinking	☐	☐
	☐	☐

Reflection:
My reflections for today:_____

_____

_____

_____

_____

_____

Quote:
My quote for today:_____

_____

> *Grace is like sunlight. Grace illuminates*
> *every corner. We just have to open the windows.*

Any additional thoughts?

_____

_____

_____

_____

_____

_____

_____

_____

_____

_____

_____

_____

_____

_____

_____

_____

_____

_____

_____

Unblemished

One year had passed since I had last seen Dylan. He had relocated to Arkansas to be closer to his family. Once in a while I wondered how he was doing and if he was still around. One day I received a letter in my mailbox. It was from Trish. I hurriedly opened and read her note.

Dear Dr. Sood,
I don't know if you remember me. I met you with my husband Dylan. He passed away six months ago.
Dylan and I met when we were both 14. He had a way of attracting stress all his life. But I must say that I had never seen him more peaceful and content than he was in his last six months. He took your message of gratitude, compassion and forgiveness to heart. He lived and surely left memories of thirty years in his last six months. He found his Christ.
I will forever be grateful to you. Know that I am both sad and happy. I miss Dylan, but promised him that I will keep myself happy. I am keeping my promise.
Blessings to you.
Trish.

I felt sad and happy reading Trish's letter. I remembered the last time I saw Dylan. He looked considerably weaker but had peace on his face. I asked him how he was handling the stress. He said something like, "My mind is stressed doctor, but my soul is not. I know better than I have ever known that my journey isn't that of body and mind alone, it is the journey of my soul. I wish I didn't have to get cancer to realize this. But so be it. I have no fear. I know where I am going. I have my work cut out for me."

He had absolutely no doubt. He was speaking from a place of knowing.

"That sure is an unblemished soul," I thought.

No diagnosis could have ever touched Dylan's soul, or for that matter can touch any soul, including yours and mine. Our inner being remains unblemished...always.

136

Additional Resources

Books: *SMART: Stress Management and Resilience Training*
          Mayo Clinic Guide to Stress Free Living
          Mayo Clinic Handbook for Happiness
          Immerse: A 52-Week Course in Resilient Living
          Mindfulness Redesigned for the Twenty-First Century
          Stronger: The Science and Art of Stress Resilience

Websites: Resilientoption.com
             Resiliencetrainer.com

Digital program: Resilientliving.net

Social Media: @amitsoodmd

References

1.   Stonnington CM, Darby B, Santucci A, et al. A resilience intervention involving mindfulness training for transplant patients and their caregivers. Clinical transplantation 2016;30:1466-72.

2.   Sood A, Sharma V, Schroeder DR, Gorman B. Stress Management and Resiliency Training (SMART) program among Department of Radiology faculty: a pilot randomized clinical trial. Explore (New York, NY) 2014;10:358-63.

3.   Sood A, Prasad K, Schroeder D, Varkey P. Stress management and resilience training among Department of Medicine faculty: a pilot randomized clinical trial. Journal of general internal medicine 2011;26:858-61.

4.   Sharma V, Sood A, Prasad K, Loehrer L, Schroeder D, Brent B. Bibliotherapy to decrease stress and anxiety and increase resilience and mindfulness: a pilot trial. Explore (New York, NY) 2014;10:248-52.

5.   Prasad K, Wahner-Roedler DL, Cha SS, Sood A. Effect of a single-session meditation training to reduce stress and improve quality of life among health care professionals: a "dose-ranging" feasibility study. Alternative therapies in health and medicine 2011;17:46-9.

6.   Magtibay DL, Chesak SS, Coughlin K, Sood A. Decreasing Stress and Burnout in Nurses: Efficacy of Blended Learning With Stress Management and Resilience Training Program. The Journal of nursing administration 2017;47:391-5.

7.   Loprinzi CE, Prasad K, Schroeder DR, Sood A. Stress Management and Resilience Training (SMART) program to decrease stress and enhance resilience among breast cancer survivors: a pilot randomized clinical trial. Clinical breast cancer 2011;11:364-8.

8.   Kashani K, Carrera P, De Moraes AG, Sood A, Onigkeit JA, Ramar K. Stress and burnout among critical care fellows: preliminary evaluation of an educational intervention. Medical education online 2015;20:27840.

9.   Chesak SS, Morin KH, Cutshall S, et al. Stress Management and Resiliency Training in a Nurse Residency Program: Findings From Participant Focus Groups. Journal for nurses in professional development 2019;35:337-43.

10.   Chesak SS, Khalsa TK, Bhagra A, Jenkins SM, Bauer BA, Sood A. Stress Management and Resiliency Training for public school teachers and staff: A novel intervention to enhance resilience and positively impact student interactions. Complementary therapies in clinical practice 2019;37:32-8.

11.   Chesak SS, Bhagra A, Schroeder DR, Foy DA, Cutshall SM, Sood A. Enhancing resilience among new nurses: feasibility and efficacy of a pilot intervention. The Ochsner journal 2015;15:38-44.

12.   Bhagra A, Medina-Inojosa JR, Vinnakota S, et al. Stress Management and Resilience Intervention in a Women's Heart Clinic: A Pilot Study. Journal of women's health (2002) 2019.

13.   Berkland BE, Werneburg BL, Jenkins SM, et al. A Worksite Wellness Intervention: Improving Happiness, Life Satisfaction, and Gratitude in Health Care Workers Improving Resiliency in Healthcare Employees. Mayo Clinic proceedings Innovations, quality & outcomes 2017;1:203-10.

14.   Otto AK, Szczesny EC, Soriano EC, Laurenceau JP, Siegel SD. Effects of a randomized gratitude intervention on death-related fear of recurrence in breast cancer

survivors. Health psychology : official journal of the Division of Health Psychology, American Psychological Association 2016;35:1320-8.

15.   Alkozei A, Smith R, Kotzin MD, Waugaman DL, Killgore WDS. The Association Between Trait Gratitude and Self-Reported Sleep Quality Is Mediated by Depressive Mood State. Behavioral sleep medicine 2019;17:41-8.

16.   Althaus B, Borasio GD, Bernard M. Gratitude at the End of Life: A Promising Lead for Palliative Care. Journal of palliative medicine 2018;21:1566-72.

17.   Sztachanska J, Krejtz I, Nezlek JB. Using a Gratitude Intervention to Improve the Lives of Women With Breast Cancer: A Daily Diary Study. Frontiers in psychology 2019;10:1365.

18.   Cunha LF, Pellanda LC, Reppold CT. Positive Psychology and Gratitude Interventions: A Randomized Clinical Trial. Frontiers in psychology 2019;10:584.

19.   Karlsson E, Andersson K, Ahlstrom BH. Loneliness despite the presence of others - adolescents' experiences of having a parent who becomes ill with cancer. European journal of oncology nursing : the official journal of European Oncology Nursing Society 2013;17:697-703.

20.   Gray TF, Azizoddin DR, Nersesian PV. Loneliness among cancer caregivers: A narrative review. Palliative & supportive care 2019:1-9.

21.   Leigh-Hunt N, Bagguley D, Bash K, et al. An overview of systematic reviews on the public health consequences of social isolation and loneliness. Public health 2017;152:157-71.

22.   Hill EM, Hamm A, Adams RN, et al. Intolerance of uncertainty, social support, and loneliness in relation to anxiety and depressive symptoms among women diagnosed with ovarian cancer
Cancer-related loneliness mediates the relationships between social constraints and symptoms among cancer patients. Psycho-oncology 2019;28:553-60.

23.   Jaremka LM, Peng J, Bornstein R, et al. Cognitive problems among breast cancer survivors: loneliness enhances risk. Psycho-oncology 2014;23:1356-64.

24.   Frinking E, Jans-Beken L, Janssens M, et al. Gratitude and loneliness in adults over 40 years: examining the role of psychological flexibility and engaged living. Aging & mental health 2019:1-8.

25.   Bartlett MY, Arpin SN. Gratitude and Loneliness: Enhancing Health and Well-Being in Older Adults. Research on aging 2019;41:772-93.

26.   Alias A, Henry M. Psychosocial Effects of Head and Neck Cancer. Oral and maxillofacial surgery clinics of North America 2018;30:499-512.

27.   Sun L, Ang E, Ang WHD, Lopez V. Losing the breast: A meta-synthesis of the impact in women breast cancer survivors. Psycho-oncology 2018;27:376-85.

28.   Izydorczyk B, Kwapniewska A, Lizinczyk S, Sitnik-Warchulska K. Psychological Resilience as a Protective Factor for the Body Image in Post-Mastectomy Women with Breast Cancer. International journal of environmental research and public health 2018;15.

29.   Seekis V, Bradley GL, Duffy A. The effectiveness of self-compassion and self-esteem writing tasks in reducing body image concerns. Body image 2017;23:206-13.

30.   Rodgers RF, Franko DL, Donovan E, et al. Body image in emerging adults: The protective role of self-compassion. Body image 2017;22:148-55.

31. Moffitt RL, Neumann DL, Williamson SP. Comparing the efficacy of a brief self-esteem and self-compassion intervention for state body dissatisfaction and self-improvement motivation. Body image 2018;27:67-76.

32. Homan KJ, Sedlak BL, Boyd EA. Gratitude buffers the adverse effect of viewing the thin ideal on body dissatisfaction. Body image 2014;11:245-50.

33. Wolfe WL, Patterson K. Comparison of a gratitude-based and cognitive restructuring intervention for body dissatisfaction and dysfunctional eating behavior in college women. Eating disorders 2017;25:330-44.

34. Bartlett MY, Valdesolo P, Arpin SN. The paradox of power: The relationship between self-esteem and gratitude. The Journal of social psychology 2019:1-12.

35. Park Y, Impett EA, MacDonald G, Lemay EP. Saying "thank you": Partners' expressions of gratitude protect relationship satisfaction and commitment from the harmful effects of attachment insecurity. Journal of personality and social psychology 2019;117:773-806.

36. Park Y, Johnson MD, MacDonald G, Impett EA. Perceiving gratitude from a romantic partner predicts decreases in attachment anxiety. Developmental psychology 2019.

37. Algoe SB, Stanton AL. Gratitude when it is needed most: social functions of gratitude in women with metastatic breast cancer. Emotion (Washington, DC) 2012;12:163-8.

38. Lambert NM, Clark MS, Durtschi J, Fincham FD, Graham SM. Benefits of expressing gratitude: expressing gratitude to a partner changes one's view of the relationship. Psychological science 2010;21:574-80.

39. Riskin A, Bamberger P, Erez A, et al. Expressions of Gratitude and Medical Team Performance. Pediatrics 2019;143.

40. Gino F, Schweitzer ME. Blinded by anger or feeling the love: how emotions influence advice taking. The Journal of applied psychology 2008;93:1165-73.

41. Konig S, Gluck J. "Gratitude is with me all the time": how gratitude relates to wisdom. The journals of gerontology Series B, Psychological sciences and social sciences 2014;69:655-66.

42. Algoe SB, Fredrickson BL, Gable SL. The social functions of the emotion of gratitude via expression. Emotion (Washington, DC) 2013;13:605-9.

43. Lambert NM, Fincham FD. Expressing gratitude to a partner leads to more relationship maintenance behavior. Emotion (Washington, DC) 2011;11:52-60.

44. Hartanto A, Lee STH, Yong JC. Dispositional Gratitude Moderates the Association between Socioeconomic Status and Interleukin-6. Scientific reports 2019;9:802.

45. Jia L, Lee LN, Tong EM. Gratitude facilitates behavioral mimicry. Emotion (Washington, DC) 2015;15:134-8.

46. Chartrand TL, Lakin JL. The antecedents and consequences of human behavioral mimicry. Annual review of psychology 2013;64:285-308.

47. DeSteno D, Duong F, Lim D, Kates S. The Grateful Don't Cheat: Gratitude as a Fount of Virtue. Psychological science 2019;30:979-88.

48. Lambert NM, Fincham FD, Stillman TF. Gratitude and depressive symptoms: the role of positive reframing and positive emotion. Cognition & emotion 2012;26:615-33.

49. O'Connell BH, Killeen-Byrt M. Psychosocial health mediates the gratitude-physical health link. Psychology, health & medicine 2018;23:1145-50.

50. Redwine LS, Henry BL, Pung MA, et al. Pilot Randomized Study of a Gratitude Journaling Intervention on Heart Rate Variability and Inflammatory Biomarkers in Patients With Stage B Heart Failure. Psychosomatic medicine 2016;78:667-76.

51. Zahn R, Moll J, Paiva M, et al. The neural basis of human social values: evidence from functional MRI. Cerebral cortex (New York, NY : 1991) 2009;19:276-83.

52. Zahn R, Garrido G, Moll J, Grafman J. Individual differences in posterior cortical volume correlate with proneness to pride and gratitude. Social cognitive and affective neuroscience 2014;9:1676-83.

53. Kong F, Zhao J, You X, Xiang Y. Gratitude and the brain: Trait gratitude mediates the association between structural variations in the medial prefrontal cortex and life satisfaction. Emotion (Washington, DC) 2019.

54. Moieni M, Irwin MR, Haltom KEB, et al. Exploring the role of gratitude and support-giving on inflammatory outcomes
The benefits of receiving gratitude for helpers: A daily investigation of proactive and reactive helping at work. Emotion (Washington, DC) 2019;19:939-49.

55. Yost-Dubrow R, Dunham Y. Evidence for a relationship between trait gratitude and prosocial behaviour. Cognition & emotion 2018;32:397-403.

56. Takahashi H, Kato M, Matsuura M, Mobbs D, Suhara T, Okubo Y. When your gain is my pain and your pain is my gain: neural correlates of envy and schadenfreude. Science (New York, NY) 2009;323:937-9.

57. Mujcic R, Oswald AJ. Is envy harmful to a society's psychological health and wellbeing? A longitudinal study of 18,000 adults. Social science & medicine (1982) 2018;198:103-11.

58. Xiang Y, Chao X, Ye Y. Effect of Gratitude on Benign and Malicious Envy: The Mediating Role of Social Support. Frontiers in psychiatry 2018;9:139.

59. Stieger M, Hill PL, Allemand M. Looking on the bright side of life: Gratitude and experiences of interpersonal transgressions in adulthood and daily life. Journal of personality 2019.

60. Chopik WJ, Newton NJ, Ryan LH, Kashdan TB, Jarden AJ. Gratitude across the life span: Age differences and links to subjective well-being. The journal of positive psychology 2019;14:292-302.

61. Aparicio M, Centeno C, Julia G, Arantzamendi M. Gratitude from patients and relatives in palliative care-characteristics and impact: a national survey. BMJ supportive & palliative care 2019.

62. Wilson TD, Reinhard DA, Westgate EC, et al. Social psychology. Just think: the challenges of the disengaged mind. Science (New York, NY) 2014;345:75-7.

63. Oudeyer PY, Kaplan F. What is Intrinsic Motivation? A Typology of Computational Approaches. Frontiers in neurorobotics 2007;1:6.

64. Kashdan TB, McKnight PE, Fincham FD, Rose P. When curiosity breeds intimacy: taking advantage of intimacy opportunities and transforming boring conversations. Journal of personality 2011;79:1369-402.

65. Stare CJ, Gruber MJ, Nadel L, Ranganath C, Gomez RL. Curiosity-driven memory enhancement persists over time but does not benefit from post-learning sleep. Cognitive neuroscience 2018;9:100-15.

66. Galli G, Sirota M, Gruber MJ, et al. Learning facts during aging: the benefits of curiosity. Experimental aging research 2018;44:311-28.

67. McGillivray S, Murayama K, Castel AD. Thirst for knowledge: The effects of curiosity and interest on memory in younger and older adults. Psychology and aging 2015;30:835-41.

68. Sakaki M, Yagi A, Murayama K. Curiosity in old age: A possible key to achieving adaptive aging. Neuroscience and biobehavioral reviews 2018;88:106-16.

69. Kang MJ, Hsu M, Krajbich IM, et al. The wick in the candle of learning: epistemic curiosity activates reward circuitry and enhances memory. Psychological science 2009;20:963-73.

70. Kaneko M, Ozaki Y, Horike K. Curiosity about a positive or negative event prolongs the duration of emotional experience. Cognition & emotion 2018;32:600-7.

71. Denneson LM, Smolenski DJ, Bush NE, Dobscha SK. Curiosity improves coping efficacy and reduces suicidal ideation severity among military veterans at risk for suicide. Psychiatry research 2017;249:125-31.

72. Beauchemin KM, Hays P. Sunny hospital rooms expedite recovery from severe and refractory depressions. Journal of affective disorders 1996;40:49-51.

73. Swan GE, Carmelli D. Curiosity and mortality in aging adults: a 5-year follow-up of the Western Collaborative Group Study. Psychology and aging 1996;11:449-53.

74. Rohrer JM, Richter D, Brummer M, Wagner GG, Schmukle SC. Successfully Striving for Happiness: Socially Engaged Pursuits Predict Increases in Life Satisfaction. Psychological science 2018;29:1291-8.

75. Poerio GL, Totterdell P, Emerson LM, Miles E. Love is the triumph of the imagination: Daydreams about significant others are associated with increased happiness, love and connection. Consciousness and cognition 2015;33:135-44.

76. Uchino BN, Trettevik R, Kent de Grey RG, Cronan S, Hogan J, Baucom BRW. Social support, social integration, and inflammatory cytokines: A meta-analysis. Health psychology : official journal of the Division of Health Psychology, American Psychological Association 2018;37:462-71.

77. Kim ES, Park N, Peterson C. Perceived neighborhood social cohesion and stroke. Social science & medicine (1982) 2013;97:49-55.

78. Kim ES, Hawes AM, Smith J. Perceived neighbourhood social cohesion and myocardial infarction. Journal of epidemiology and community health 2014;68:1020-6.

79. Kershaw KN, Diez Roux AV, Bertoni A, Carnethon MR, Everson-Rose SA, Liu K. Associations of chronic individual-level and neighbourhood-level stressors with incident coronary heart disease: the Multi-Ethnic Study of Atherosclerosis. Journal of epidemiology and community health 2015;69:136-41.

80. Strom JL, Egede LE. The impact of social support on outcomes in adult patients with type 2 diabetes: a systematic review. Current diabetes reports 2012;12:769-81.

81. Mookadam F, Arthur HM. Social support and its relationship to morbidity and mortality after acute myocardial infarction: systematic overview. Archives of internal medicine 2004;164:1514-8.

82. Stormer VS, Alvarez GA. Attention Alters Perceived Attractiveness. Psychological science 2016;27:563-71.

83.   Fredrickson BL. Updated thinking on positivity ratios. The American psychologist 2013;68:814-22.
84.   Liberman Z, Shaw A. Secret to friendship: Children make inferences about friendship based on secret sharing. Developmental psychology 2018;54:2139-51.
85.   Slepian ML, Masicampo EJ, Toosi NR, Ambady N. The physical burdens of secrecy. Journal of experimental psychology General 2012;141:619-24.
86.   Laird RD, Bridges BJ, Marsee MA. Secrets from friends and parents: longitudinal links with depression and antisocial behavior. Journal of adolescence 2013;36:685-93.
87.   Kawamichi H, Yoshihara K, Sasaki AT, et al. Perceiving active listening activates the reward system and improves the impression of relevant experiences. Social neuroscience 2015;10:16-26.
88.   Roter DL, Frankel RM, Hall JA, Sluyter D. The expression of emotion through nonverbal behavior in medical visits. Mechanisms and outcomes. Journal of general internal medicine 2006;21 Suppl 1:S28-34.
89.   Singh C, Leder D. Touch in the consultation. The British journal of general practice : the journal of the Royal College of General Practitioners 2012;62:147-8.
90.   Osmun WE, Brown JB, Stewart M, Graham S. Patients' attitudes to comforting touch in family practice. Canadian family physician Medecin de famille canadien 2000;46:2411-6.
91.   Debrot A, Schoebi D, Perrez M, Horn AB. Touch as an interpersonal emotion regulation process in couples' daily lives: the mediating role of psychological intimacy. Personality & social psychology bulletin 2013;39:1373-85.
92.   Holt-Lunstad J, Birmingham WA, Light KC. Influence of a "warm touch" support enhancement intervention among married couples on ambulatory blood pressure, oxytocin, alpha amylase, and cortisol. Psychosomatic medicine 2008;70:976-85.
93.   Grewen KM, Anderson BJ, Girdler SS, Light KC. Warm partner contact is related to lower cardiovascular reactivity. Behavioral medicine (Washington, DC) 2003;29:123-30.
94.   von Mohr M, Kirsch LP, Fotopoulou A. The soothing function of touch: affective touch reduces feelings of social exclusion. Scientific reports 2017;7:13516.
95.   Hertenstein MJ, Holmes R, McCullough M, Keltner D. The communication of emotion via touch. Emotion (Washington, DC) 2009;9:566-73.
96.   Kraus MW, Huang C, Keltner D. Tactile communication, cooperation, and performance: an ethological study of the NBA. Emotion (Washington, DC) 2010;10:745-9.
97.   Little P, White P, Kelly J, Everitt H, Mercer S. Randomised controlled trial of a brief intervention targeting predominantly non-verbal communication in general practice consultations. The British journal of general practice : the journal of the Royal College of General Practitioners 2015;65:e351-6.
98.   Inagaki TK, Eisenberger NI. Shared neural mechanisms underlying social warmth and physical warmth. Psychological science 2013;24:2272-80.
99.   Weng HY, Fox AS, Shackman AJ, et al. Compassion training alters altruism and neural responses to suffering. Psychological science 2013;24:1171-80.
100.   Breines JG, Thoma MV, Gianferante D, Hanlin L, Chen X, Rohleder N. Self-compassion as a predictor of interleukin-6 response to acute psychosocial stress. Brain, behavior, and immunity 2014;37:109-14.

101. Pace TW, Negi LT, Dodson-Lavelle B, et al. Engagement with Cognitively-Based Compassion Training is associated with reduced salivary C-reactive protein from before to after training in foster care program adolescents. Psychoneuroendocrinology 2013;38:294-9.

102. Hein G, Silani G, Preuschoff K, Batson CD, Singer T. Neural responses to ingroup and outgroup members' suffering predict individual differences in costly helping. Neuron 2010;68:149-60.

103. Young SG, Hugenberg K. Mere social categorization modulates identification of facial expressions of emotion. Journal of personality and social psychology 2010;99:964-77.

104. Diedrich A, Grant M, Hofmann SG, Hiller W, Berking M. Self-compassion as an emotion regulation strategy in major depressive disorder. Behaviour research and therapy 2014;58:43-51.

105. Rakel D, Barrett B, Zhang Z, et al. Perception of empathy in the therapeutic encounter: effects on the common cold. Patient education and counseling 2011;85:390-7.

106. Surakka V, Hietanen JK. Facial and emotional reactions to Duchenne and non-Duchenne smiles. International journal of psychophysiology : official journal of the International Organization of Psychophysiology 1998;29:23-33.

107. Barreto SM. Why does happiness matter? Understanding the relation between positive emotion and health outcomes. Social science & medicine (1982) 2017;191:61-4.

108. Shore DM, Heerey EA. The value of genuine and polite smiles. Emotion (Washington, DC) 2011;11:169-74.

109. Bernhardt BC, Singer T. The neural basis of empathy. Annual review of neuroscience 2012;35:1-23.

110. Akitsuki Y, Decety J. Social context and perceived agency affects empathy for pain: an event-related fMRI investigation. NeuroImage 2009;47:722-34.

111. Lamm C, Batson CD, Decety J. The neural substrate of human empathy: effects of perspective-taking and cognitive appraisal. Journal of cognitive neuroscience 2007;19:42-58.

112. Meyer ML, Masten CL, Ma Y, et al. Empathy for the social suffering of friends and strangers recruits distinct patterns of brain activation. Social cognitive and affective neuroscience 2013;8:446-54.

113. Zheng L, Wang Q, Cheng X, et al. Perceived reputation of others modulates empathic neural responses. Experimental brain research 2016;234:125-32.

114. Bremner RH, Koole SL, Bushman BJ. "Pray for those who mistreat you": effects of prayer on anger and aggression. Personality & social psychology bulletin 2011;37:830-7.

115. Desbordes G, Negi LT, Pace TW, Wallace BA, Raison CL, Schwartz EL. Effects of mindful-attention and compassion meditation training on amygdala response to emotional stimuli in an ordinary, non-meditative state. Frontiers in human neuroscience 2012;6:292.

116. Hutcherson CA, Seppala EM, Gross JJ. Loving-kindness meditation increases social connectedness. Emotion (Washington, DC) 2008;8:720-4.

117. Kang Y, Gray JR, Dovidio JF. The nondiscriminating heart: lovingkindness meditation training decreases implicit intergroup bias. Journal of experimental psychology General 2014;143:1306-13.

118. Lumma AL, Kok BE, Singer T. Is meditation always relaxing? Investigating heart rate, heart rate variability, experienced effort and likeability during training of three types of meditation. International journal of psychophysiology : official journal of the International Organization of Psychophysiology 2015;97:38-45.

119. Sheng F, Han S. Manipulations of cognitive strategies and intergroup relationships reduce the racial bias in empathic neural responses. NeuroImage 2012;61:786-97.

120. Sheng F, Liu Q, Li H, Fang F, Han S. Task modulations of racial bias in neural responses to others' suffering. NeuroImage 2014;88:263-70.

121. Bucchioni G, Lelard T, Ahmaidi S, Godefroy O, Krystkowiak P, Mouras H. Do we feel the same empathy for loved and hated peers? PloS one 2015;10:e0125871.

122. Guadagni V, Burles F, Ferrara M, Iaria G. The effects of sleep deprivation on emotional empathy. Journal of sleep research 2014;23:657-63.

123. Sheeran P, Gollwitzer PM, Bargh JA. Nonconscious processes and health. Health psychology : official journal of the Division of Health Psychology, American Psychological Association 2013;32:460-73.

124. Gable SL, Reis HT, Impett EA, Asher ER. What do you do when things go right? The intrapersonal and interpersonal benefits of sharing positive events. Journal of personality and social psychology 2004;87:228-45.

125. McCullough ME, Fincham FD, Tsang JA. Forgiveness, forbearance, and time: the temporal unfolding of transgression-related interpersonal motivations. Journal of personality and social psychology 2003;84:540-57.

126. Toussaint L, Kamble S, Marschall JC, Duggi DB. The effects of brief prayer on the experience of forgiveness: An American and Indian comparison. International journal of psychology : Journal international de psychologie 2016;51:288-95.

Acknowledgments

I am grateful to the countless scientists, reporters, philosophers, and authors who have helped me learn the information I share in this book.

I am grateful to every person who has helped me smile, smiled at my sometimes not-so-funny jokes, and helped me keep a light heart.

I am grateful to my parents, Sahib and Shashi; my in-laws, Vinod and Kusum; my brothers, Kishore and Sundeep; my sisters, Sandhya, Rajni, and Smita; our extended family members; my daughters, Gauri and Sia; and my wife, Richa, for showering me with love that sustains me every day.

I am grateful to all my friends and colleagues for their support and love.

I am grateful to all my students and patients who trust my values and my ability to be of help. You give me strength every single day.

I am grateful to you all for helping build a kinder, happier, and more hopeful world for our planet's children. Thank you.

Amit

About Dr. Sood

Dr. Amit Sood is married to his lovely wife of 26 years, Dr. Richa Sood. They have two girls, Gauri age 15, and Sia age 9.

Dr. Sood serves as the Executive Director of the Global Center for Resiliency and Wellbeing and The GRIT Institute. Dr. Sood is a former professor of medicine, chair of the Mind-Body Medicine Initiative, and director of student life and wellness at Mayo Clinic.

Dr. Sood completed his residency in internal medicine at the Albert Einstein School of Medicine, an integrative medicine fellowship at the University of Arizona, and earned a master's degree in clinical research from Mayo Clinic College of Medicine. He has received several National Institutes of Health grants and foundation awards to test and implement integrative and mind-body approaches within medicine.

Dr. Sood has developed an innovative approach toward mind-body medicine by incorporating concepts from neuroscience, evolutionary biology, psychology, philosophy, and spirituality. His resulting program, Stress Management and Resiliency Training (SMART©) helps patients learn skills to decrease stress and enhance resiliency by improving self-awareness, engagement, and emotional resilience. Interventions adapted from the program reach approximately 50,000 patients and learners each year. The program has been tested in over 30 clinical trials.

Dr. Sood's programs are offered for a wide variety of patients and learners according to their unique needs, including to improve resiliency; decrease stress and anxiety; enhance well-being and happiness; provide relief and prevention of cancer symptoms; and as wellness solutions for caregivers, corporate executives, health care professionals, parents, and students. The SMART© program is now integrated into several hospitals and health systems and is used for managing burnout, leadership training, and enhancing resilience among nurses. It is being offered with all ages of students, and teachers.

Dr. Sood has authored or co-authored over 70 peer-reviewed articles, and several editorials, book chapters, abstracts, and letters. Dr. Sood is the author of the books *SMART with Dr. Sood, The Mayo Clinic Guide to Stress-Free Living, The Mayo Clinic Handbook for Happiness, Immerse: A 52-Week Course in Resilient Living, Stronger: The Science and Art of Stress Resilience, Mindfulness Redesigned for the Twenty-First Century, and Build Your Immune Resilience.* As an international expert in his field, Dr. Sood's work has been widely cited in the press including *The Atlantic Monthly, USA Today, Wall Street Journal, New York Times, NPR, Reuters Health, Time Magazine (online), Good Housekeeping, Parenting, Real Simple, Shape, US News, Huffington Post, Men's Health Magazine, The Globe and Mail, CBS News, Fox News, and others.* He has interviewed with several prominent TV and radio shows, both nationally and internationally. He was selected as one of the 2015 Health care Pioneers by the Robert Wood Johnson Foundation.

He is a highly sought-after speaker, and delivered the TEDx talk – *Happy Brain: How to Overcome Our Neural Predispositions to Suffering.* He has mentored several hundred fellows, medical students, instructors, consultants, and residents. Dr. Sood is currently working with several large hospitals and health systems, as well as Fortune 500 companies to implement his solutions for employee wellbeing. He is currently training about 150 students to become certified resilience trainers through his CeRT (Certified Resilience Trainer) program (resiliencetrainer.com).

Dr. Sood has received several awards for his work, including the Mayo Clinic's 2010 Distinguished Service Award, Mayo's 2010 Innovator of the Year Award, and 2013 outstanding physician scientist award. He was chosen as one among the top 20 intelligent optimists "helping the world be a better place" by *Ode Magazine.*

Dr. Sood serves on the Wellbeing Advisory Board of Everyday Health.

Made in the USA
Las Vegas, NV
06 January 2024

84010717R00085